HOW TO
photograph
cars

HOW TO
photograph
cars

The enthusiast's guide to techniques and equipment

TONY BAKER

Haynes Publishing

First published in November 2002

A catalogue record for this book is available from the British Library

ISBN 1 85960 855 8

Library of Congress catalog card no. 2001099297

Published by Haynes Publishing, Sparkford, Yeovil, Somerset, BA22 7JJ, UK

Tel: 01963 442030 Fax: 01963 440001
Int. tel: +44 1963 442030 Int. fax: +44 1963 440001
E-mail: sales@haynes-manuals.co.uk
Web site: www.haynes.co.uk

Haynes North America, Inc.,
861 Lawrence Drive, Newbury Park,
California 91320, USA

Printed and bound in England by
J. H. Haynes & Co. Ltd, Sparkford

Acknowledgements

Most of the pictures in this book are © Tony Baker/*Classic & Sports Car* and are reproduced by kind permission of the magazine. The exceptions are as follows:

Page 4 © Neil Godwin-Stubbert.
Page 20 (Ferrari F2001), © Steven Tee/LAT.
Page 30 (Jordan EJ11), © Steven Tee/LAT.
Page 53 (Opel Manta), © Tony Baker.

Page 86 (Mazda MX-5), © Tony Baker.
Page 90 (McLaren MP4 16), © Martyn Elford/LAT.
Page 92 (Touring Cars), © Malcolm Griffiths/LAT.
Page 94 (Audi R8), © Lorenzo Bellanca/LAT.
Page 95 (Touring Cars) © Malcolm Griffiths/LAT.
Page 97 (Hyundai Accent), © McKlein/LAT.
Page 101 (Jaguar XK140 Roadster) © Tony Baker.
Pages 154–155 (all three pictures) © James Mann/*Classic & Sports Car*.

Contents

Introduction

Cars are a natural choice of subject for the keen photographer. They are designed to be visually appealing, with sleek curves and aerodynamic profiles. They are often brightly coloured, and adorned with shiny chrome and attractive detailing. They can, up to a point, be moved to the photographer's choice of location, or shot on the move to create dramatic action pictures. Motorsport also provides a thrilling spectacle full of opportunities to create exciting images. Yet many of us, whether we are photographers or car enthusiasts, find it difficult to produce pleasing car pictures and are left disappointed by our results.

The aim of this book is to explain how anyone can take great photographs of cars. There is no mystery to the process, although, as with all photography, a little technical knowledge is useful. More important, though, are careful planning, an awareness of light and weather, and an 'eye' for a good photograph, and these are the areas in which successful photographers excel.

◁ Both action and static photography require advance planning. Although each calls for different techniques, careful attention has to be paid to the choice of location, to the weather, the time of day and the likely lighting conditions. For this Alfa Giulia shot, the driver moved the car into position while I looked through the camera's viewfinder and minute adjustments were made until a pleasing composition was achieved. It was then a matter of waiting until the lighting conditions were perfect, and this is where patience is necessary – sometimes a long wait produces far better pictures than a hasty approach.
Alfa Giulia SS, near Epping Forest, Essex, England. Mamiya RB67 camera, 65mm lens, graduated grey and 85B warm-up filters, Fuji Velvia.

△For this Fiat Dino, a stretch of quiet road with an uncluttered background was chosen, and the pictures were shot at a time when late afternoon sunlight would light the car perfectly. Inevitably, there are often situations where the photographer does not have complete control, and compromise is necessary. But for the determined photographer it is important to create the best picture possible under any set of circumstances.
Fiat Dino Spider, North York Moors, England. Canon EOS1n, 70–200mm zoom lens, Fuji Provia.

It's important to remember, too, that good photography does not require the purchase of bags full of expensive and complicated camera equipment; a creative photographer can produce stunning images with the simplest camera by making the most of the subject matter, the choice of viewpoint and the lighting conditions.

Look through almost any car magazine and you will see striking and original pictures. This book aims to provide an insight into the methods used by professional photographers to create those images, but to do so without resorting to technical language or impenetrable jargon. The basic techniques needed to take great photographs are easily understood even by those with no previous experience of the subject. Modern cameras, with automatic exposure and focusing, allow the user to concentrate on picture taking and have removed the need for detailed understanding of the technical side of photography, which many people find daunting.

Photography is not a subject that can be learned about simply by reading words; it is far more important to look carefully at examples of good photography and analyse why those pictures succeed. For that reason, much of the information on the following pages is presented in the form of captions to the pictures, to allow the reader to appreciate the ideas and techniques behind the creation of the images. And while many of the photographs here are of exotic and expensive cars, it is important to remember that the principles behind good photography remain the same whatever the subject matter.

No matter how beautiful the car is, great pictures have to be created and this is where the skill in photography lies.

△Photography is all about careful observation. Here a dramatic winter afternoon sky was reflected in the car's rear window and I chose to go in close with a wide-angle lens and make the Ferrari badge the focal point of the image.
Ferrari Daytona, near Porrentroy, Switzerland. Canon EOS1n, 24mm lens, 81A warm-up filter, Fuji Provia.

Why any camera can be used to take great pictures

It is a commonly held misconception that successful photographs can only be taken by those who own the latest sophisticated equipment. Nothing could be further from the truth: a camera is simply a tool for taking photographs in the same way that an artist's paintbrush is a tool for painting. Buy an expensive camera in the belief that it will make you a better photographer and you have wasted your money. Good photography is all about seeing, and many successful professional photographers deliberately choose simple cameras, believing that a bewildering array of features and choice of various operating modes distract from the business of picture taking.

Even if equipped with nothing more than a humble compact camera, the creative photographer will produce striking pictures. The actual act of taking a photograph is only the last stage of a process that involves careful choice of location and viewpoint, as well as use of the prevailing lighting conditions, and all of these decisions are made before the camera is even raised to the eye. Most of us own some form of 'point-and-shoot' compact camera that is simple to use and produces good photographs with minimal effort, and there is no reason why such cameras cannot be used for car photography. They allow pictures to be taken quickly and with the minimum of fuss. Using a simple camera is good discipline; it forces the user to concentrate on the subject and there are many circumstances in which the photographer fiddling with complicated equipment will miss a picture that he or she would have shot with a point-and-shoot camera.

It is important to remember, though, that the keen photographer needs to have as much control as possible over the final image and this is where basic cameras have their limitations. Most have fully automatic exposure and focus, and while this makes photography easy for users with no technical knowledge, those who are able to read situations where automation can be fooled will find the lack of input to these processes frus-

∨Here a distinctive location was chosen and the end result is again a picture that could have been taken with any camera. The car was placed at an angle that echoed the line of the viaduct as this appeared to create the most pleasing composition. Although the weather was dull this at least ensured that the car was evenly lit and the bright red colour stands out well from the background.
MG TF, Ribblehead Viaduct, Yorkshire, England. Mamiya RB67, 90mm lens, graduated grey and 81A warm-up filters, Fuji Provia.

∨To make the most of a dull day and a rather uninspiring landscape, I chose a low viewpoint, lying on the ground amongst the rocks. The out-of-focus foreground leads the viewer's eye to the car. The ability to recognise the potential of unusual locations and viewpoints is far more important than owning expensive equipment.
Alfa Romeo 8C 2900, Loch Doon, Dumfries and Galloway, Scotland. Mamiya RB67, 180mm lens, Fuji Provia.

trating. It is important that the camera user has some control over shutter speed and aperture. Correct exposure is achieved through a combination of the two, and for any form of action photography, the photographer needs to specify the shutter speed and many fully automatic cameras don't allow even this limited amount of control.

Just as importantly for the car photographer, most basic cameras do not allow the photographer to change lenses and this imposes serious limitations. In particular, if you wish to take photographs at motorsport events you will probably need to use to telephoto lenses if your end results are going to depict cars as anything more than distant specks in a landscape.

The best camera for car photography, and indeed for most photography, is the 35mm single-lens reflex (SLR) camera, or its digital equivalent. These cameras have a single lens through which the image is viewed and photographed: in other words, what you see is exactly what you get. This makes precise framing and composition easy (and makes it impossible to leave the lens cap on!) but the main advantage of this design is the ability to change lenses. This facility opens up a whole new realm of opportunities to the keen photographer.

◁ Although shot with a 35mm SLR, this striking image could have been taken with almost any camera. The wall was chosen to provide a suitable background and a time of day chosen when it would be sunlit. The car was driven up and down the road past the photographer, allowing several attempts at getting the picture. The 'highlight' on the car (the bright reflection of the sun) was a happy accident that improves the image considerably.
Porsche 944, Isleworth, Middlesex, England. Canon EOS1n, 35mm lens, Fuji Velvia.

Digital or film?

In recent years there has been a revolution in camera technology, and digital cameras capable of producing high-quality results are now widely available. As a camera buyer, you now have the choice to make: whether to use the familiar film or to embrace the new digital technology. Digital cameras do not require film, as they use a CCD (charge-coupled device) to capture the image, and this is then stored digitally on a memory card which can be re-used many times once the images have been downloaded to a computer. Both film and digital methods of image capture have much to commend them and ultimately it comes down to personal preference.

There is a vast range of film-based cameras available to suit all pockets. Compact cameras capable of producing high-quality images can be bought for just a few pounds while, for a slightly greater outlay, the keen photographer can buy an SLR camera together with a couple of lenses that will last for years and allow them to shoot almost any subject with confidence. Film choice is remarkable: there are print and transparency materials in a range of speeds (a film's speed is its sensitivity to light) that will produce pictures displaying outstanding sharpness, while black-and-white film and other more specialised materials are also widely available. Print films can be processed in about an hour by high-street outlets and, if carefully looked after, negatives and transparencies will last for a lifetime. If you're a committed photographer wishing to specialise in car photography you can choose from a variety of professional SLRs with fast motor drives and quick, accurate auto-focusing. The major camera manufacturers produce vast camera systems,

▽ This picture was shot specifically for a magazine's front cover and it was essential to take a sequence of pictures in quick succession. This is a failing of even the best digital cameras, as the camera takes time to 'save' the images to its memory card. Additionally the pictures needed to be of high resolution and even a few images like this will fill the memory card very quickly; in such circumstances film is still the best medium.
Mazda MX-5, test track at Chobham, Surrey, England. Canon EOS1n, 300mm lens, Fuji Provia.

In circumstances like this, where there is a great deal of fine detail and the car occupies only a small proportion of the frame, a digital camera would need to be used at its highest resolution and even then the finished result could not match the sharpness and colour rendition of fine-grained film.
Lancia Flaminia Sport, near Montecatini Terme, Italy. Mamiya RB67, 180mm lens, Fuji Velvia.

which include lenses of all focal lengths as well as specialised accessories that open up a whole world of possibilities. If you wish to keep expenditure down, you can choose from a wide range of second-hand equipment.

For the photographer choosing the digital route, the choice is much more limited. While digital compact cameras are now readily available, they cost significantly more than their film counterparts. The quality of a digital image relies first on the number of pixels available via the CCD (the more pixels, the better the quality of the image) and the cheaper cameras will produce results that, if you're used to looking at film images, you will find disappointing. At the other end of the scale, there are only a few professional-quality digital SLRs available and the high cost of these – they can cost ten times more than a similar film SLR – puts them outside the reach of all but the wealthiest amateur photographers. Against the higher cost of digital cameras can be

offset the fact that no film will ever be needed.

One big advantage offered by digital cameras is that the saved picture can be viewed instantly using the LCD screen on the back of the camera, and while this is a small, low-resolution image it serves as a good check on lighting, exposure and composition. Unsuccessful shots can be discarded straight away, saving space on the memory card. Digital cameras also possess the big advantage that images can be downloaded direct to a computer without the need for an additional scanning device. Pictures can then be manipulated using special software and printed using an inkjet printer; these are available for reasonable cost and produce outstanding prints for a fraction of the cost of prints made via negatives.

From the car photographer's point of view, most digital cameras suffer the disadvantage that they have limited ability to store a number of images in rapid succession, which can be a major handicap when shooting action.

When shooting tracking shots like this, most professional photographers will use a lot of film to ensure a selection of sharp images. Most of the rest will end up in the bin and this is a situation where a digital camera, which needs no film, could come in useful. However, it would be difficult to check the sharpness of the pictures while on location, (which means that a lot of large-capacity memory cards would be needed) and again the time taken to save each image may be a problem.
Ferrari 412P, test track at Chobham, Surrey, England. Canon EOS1n, 24mm lens, 81C warm-up filter, Fuji Velvia.

SLR cameras

Having declared that the 35mm SLR, or its digital equivalent, is the ideal tool for car photography some further explanation may help to clarify why. The big advantage of the SLR is the fact that the viewing and taking of the image are done through the same lens (the mirror which provides the viewfinder image flips up out of the way within a split-second of the shutter release being pressed). This means that what you see through the viewfinder is exactly what will appear on the final image. Focusing can be done accurately – if the image is sharp in the viewfinder it will be sharp in the finished picture. Filters and other accessories can be precisely adjusted to give the desired effect. The SLR also allows lenses from wide-angles to extreme telephotos to be fitted and the photographer can still view the image exactly as it will appear. The advantages of this

An SLR camera is ideal for this kind of photograph and a wide-angle lens was chosen to provide a dramatic perspective. Shooting from the back of a moving car, the cars were carefully guided into position and the shutter release pressed at the instant they formed a pleasing composition. A fast motor drive allowed a sequence of pictures to be taken during the few moments that the cars were in the right formation, which ensured a higher chance of a sharp end result than shooting just one or two frames. **Caterham 7 Superlight R500 (on left) and Lotus 7 Series 1, sprint course at Curborough, near Lichfield, England. Canon EOS1n, 24mm lens with 85B warm-up and graduated grey filters, fill-in flash, Fuji Provia.**

△ This is a picture that would have been virtually impossible to shoot on anything other than an SLR camera. All four cars needed to be carefully positioned so that they could be clearly seen, and this sort of precise framing is difficult without through-the-lens viewing. A waist-level viewfinder – a useful accessory – allowed the picture to be composed with the camera on the ground, a viewpoint that was chosen to add impact. A graduated grey filter was used to retain some tone in an otherwise blank sky, and the position of this was carefully adjusted while looking through the lens. The cars' sidelights and hazard lights were turned on to liven up the picture on a dull day. Left to right: Porsche 924, Porsche 944S2, Porsche 968 and Porsche 944, airfield at Wroughton, Wiltshire, England. Mamiya RB67 with waist-level viewfinder, 65mm lens, graduated grey filter, Fuji Provia.

for the car photographer are clear. Nearly all SLR cameras, even those with high degrees of automation, allow some input to the choice of shutter speed and aperture and this is vital for anyone who wishes to shoot action pictures.

Because the SLR is so widely used, by professional as well as amateur photographers, manufacturers have invested time and money in improving it with the result that the modern camera is a superb piece of equipment, offering a wealth of features including fast motor drives, quick and accurate auto-focusing, reliable automatic exposure with a choice of operating modes, and 'custom' functions that allow the user to specify certain settings. All of these contribute to the usefulness of the SLR camera as a tool for car photography, and for action photography in particular. The manufacturers also produce a huge range of lenses – everything from fish-eye lenses to ultra-long telephotos costing many thousands of pounds – as well a multitude of other accessories that create an entire camera 'system' and allow virtually any kind of photography to be undertaken with confidence.

If you are at all serious about the business of car photography, then an SLR camera will be a wise purchase. It is difficult to recommend any particular brand, as most modern cameras are made to high standards, but if you wish to shoot action pictures you will need to choose a model that has a fast motor drive. Auto-focusing, while

useful, is not absolutely necessary to take good action photos, although few SLRs without it are made these days. When buying a camera the old adage that 'you get what you pay for' holds true – while a professional-quality SLR represents a significant investment, it will work reliably for many years and you are unlikely to find a photographic situation that is beyond its capabilities. It is worth noting that most professional photographers, including those who specialise in cars, choose 35mm cameras made by Nikon or Canon and these companies not only make first-rate equipment but offer excellent back-up services, such as fast turn-round of repairs, that are essential for those who rely on cameras to earn their living.

Don't spend your entire budget on the camera purchase; there's no point in owning a quality SLR but not being able to afford additional lenses. Decide before you buy which lenses you are likely to want and divide up your budget accordingly.

▽ For pictures like this a long telephoto lens is essential, and no compact or rangefinder camera has a zoom lens long enough to allow shooting in safety. A fast motor drive is also necessary and only SLR cameras made for professional use offer drives with speeds of five or six frames-per-second. Committed car photographers will soon find lesser cameras frustratingly inadequate. Ferrari 328 GTS, test track at Chobham, Surrey, England. Canon EOS1n, 300mm lens, Fuji Provia.

Understanding exposure

To create successful pictures, a photographer needs to be able to specify some of the camera settings, or at least to understand enough about them to trust an automatic camera in some situations. The most important settings are those that control shutter speed and aperture. Most modern cameras have some form of fully automatic mode that takes care of both these functions, but for car photography this is largely an unsatisfactory method of working. In particular, for action photography the camera user needs to be able to specify the shutter speed so a camera that has, at the very least, some sort of shutter-priority mode is essential.

Correct exposure is achieved by a combination of shutter speed and aperture, which

Here I wanted to create a picture that had plenty of movement but still gave a distinct image of the car. I opted for a shutter speed of 1/8th of a second, to provide the necessary blur to the background, but then added a burst of flash to retain detail in the front of the car. Pictures like this are difficult to achieve with fully automatic cameras.
Ferrari 330P, San Marino. Canon EOS1n, 24mm lens, Metz 60CT-4 flash, Fuji Velvia.

This picture illustrates why it is essential to have some control over the camera settings: dark vegetation like that in the background will almost always fool a camera's meter into over-exposing. By taking a separate exposure reading and transferring those settings to the camera I was able to ensure that the exposure was accurate, and I needed to be able to select a shutter speed of 1/60th of a second to create the impression of movement. **Aston Martin DB4 GT Zagato Sanction II, near Chichester, West Sussex, England. Canon EOS1n, 70–200mm zoom lens, Fuji Velvia.**

between them control the amount of light that reaches the film. Virtually all cameras have an exposure meter within them that will either control the exposure automatically or suggest the correct settings to the user. Shutter speed is the length of time that light falls on the film, while aperture is the size of the hole through which the light passes. A fast shutter speed will need a wide aperture to give correct exposure, while a long shutter speed will allow a smaller aperture to be used. Exposure is talked of in terms of 'stops'; a one-stop increase in exposure means that twice as much light is reaching the film, whether via a longer shutter speed or a wider aperture. Shutter speeds follow the sequence 1/1000th of a second, 1/500sec, 1/250sec, 1/125sec, 1/60sec, 1/30sec, 1/15sec, 1/8sec, 1/4sec and so on, while apertures follow the sequence f/2.8, f/4, f/5.6, f/8, f/11, f/16, f/22. Each of these settings is a difference of one stop from the preceding or succeeding one, and a one-stop decrease in aperture requires a one-stop increase in shutter speed. This means that an exposure of 1/60sec at f/8 is exactly the same as an exposure of 1/125sec at f/5.6. (Many cam-

eras allow the photographer to make half-stop adjustments to exposure, giving a greater degree of control.)

In addition to controlling the amount of light reaching the film, the lens aperture makes a difference to the depth-of-field. In simple terms this is the amount of the subject that is in focus. Small apertures give greater depth-of-field (that is, more of the subject is in focus) while wide apertures reduce the depth-of-field. This is why it is so important for the photographer to understand and appreciate these camera controls; to create an exciting action shot you may need to set a shutter speed of 1/60th of a second but you will need to be aware of the difference this may make to the depth-of-field.

The other factor that has a bearing on exposure is the sensitivity, or 'speed' of the film. Fast films are very sensitive and allow the photographer to select fast shutter speeds or small lens apertures, but tend to produce images of inferior quality to those shot on slower, less sensitive films. Most professional photographers will choose to use slow films wherever possible as image quality is often of prime importance.

Unusual lighting conditions like this always require the photographer to understand and appreciate exposure and film; it was important to work quickly as the light levels fell and the bright sky would have led the camera's exposure meter to under-expose the car. I used a graduated filter to reduce the contrast between the bright sky and the foreground. **Morgan Plus 8, Malvern Hills, Worcestershire, England. Mamiya RB67, 65mm lens, graduated grey and 85B warm-up filters, Fuji Provia.**

Auto-focus

One of the most difficult aspects of action photography is ensuring sharp focus of fast-moving objects. Before the advent of automatic focusing, the photographer shooting a moving car had to pre-focus the camera and then hope to hit the shutter button a split second before the car reached the point of focus, thus allowing time for the camera's mirror to flip up before the shutter actually opened. It was a technique that required a great deal of practice and even then success wasn't guaranteed.

Nowadays virtually every camera, whether a compact or an SLR, features automatic focusing as standard, and it is easy to assume that this is the answer to the action photographer's prayers.

This isn't always the case, but let's start by emphasising the positive aspects of this technology. The biggest advantage of automatic focusing it that it removes one of the most difficult technical considerations, allowing the photographer to concentrate on the subject. In particular, shooting motorsport has been made very much easier; most quality SLRs now have an auto-focus mode that is specifically designed for moving subjects, and good auto-focusing can keep up with even a fast-moving car. The particular advantage of this is that a sequence of sharp images can be shot whereas the pre-focus technique gave – at best – only one sharp shot.

You can shoot a car as it passes all the way

Automatic focusing has made motorsport photography very much easier: the photographer can concentrate on the action and shoot at exactly the right moment, confident that the camera will take care of sharpness. Here the lettering and numbers on the side of the car gave plenty of contrast for the auto-focus to 'find'. **Alfa Romeo GTA replica, Nürburgring, Germany. Canon EOS1n, 70–200mm zoom lens, Fuji Provia.**

Effective automatic focusing will keep track of a moving subject, even one that is quickly approaching the camera. Here there was sufficient detail on the front of the car, and enough light, for the auto-focus to find and follow the car, even while shooting at the motor drive's maximum rate of six frames per second. This meant that, when examining the results, it was possible to select the final image on the basis of which was the most dramatic, as all of them were sharp.
Napier 'Samson', near Basingstoke, Hampshire, England. Canon EOS1n, 70–200mm zoom lens, Fuji Provia.

through your field of view and be reasonably sure that most will be in sharp focus.

While it is true that auto-focus has made it very much easier to photograph moving cars satisfactorily, like all technological innovations, it has its limitations. Different manufacturers use different systems but all auto-focus relies on the subject having areas of contrast on which it can focus, and car bodywork can sometimes pose a problem here. If the camera can't find sufficient levels of contrast then the auto-focus will 'hunt' throughout its focusing range and the shot will be missed. Dull days can exacerbate the problem since the inherent contrast in any subject is very much lower in these conditions.

Auto-focus also works better with lenses that have wide maximum apertures, as the extra brightness that these lenses provide makes it easier for the camera to focus on the subject. While camera manufacturers have perfected auto-focus that will keep up with an approaching car, it often struggles when shooting cars that are travelling away from the camera. There's no real solution to this and it is often best to revert to the pre-focus technique in these circumstances. Another point worth mentioning: an auto-focus SLR camera usually offers a choice of focus points that the user can select, but these are usually ranged across the middle of the viewfinder and this makes it difficult to compose a picture with, say, a moving car in the corner of the frame.

Few professional photographers will rely absolutely on automatic focusing. Most experienced car photographers will quickly recognise situations where the auto-focus will struggle and will make allowances or focus manually.

This is the type of image that auto-focus can struggle with; the front of the car is very dark and there is little in the way of contrasting detail. This is a valuable car that is difficult to manoeuvre and so only a few 'passes' could be made. Aware of the possibility that the shot could be missed, I chose to revert to the pre-focusing technique.
Bugatti Type 50, near Watlington, Oxfordshire, England. Canon EOS1n, 300mm lens, Fuji Provia.

17

Medium and large formats

If the 35mm SLR is so well suited to car photography, why do so many professional photographers choose to use larger formats? The simple answer is: image quality. For all the flexibility offered by 35mm cameras, the image size of a transparency or negative is only 36mm x 24mm and, even with today's fine-grained materials, for really first-rate reproduction or print quality larger films give noticeably better results.

All medium and large format cameras are heavier, more cumbersome and slower to use than their 35mm counterparts and aren't generally suitable for action photography. Few have automatic exposure or focusing and many have no exposure meter at all, as most professional photographers usually work with a separate meter. Most need to be used on a tripod, but this is not necessarily a disadvantage as it imposes a slower, more disciplined approach on the photographer. For the amateur photographer the biggest disadvantage of the larger formats will be the considerable extra cost, not only of the cameras and lenses but of film and processing too. If you wish to use print films in medium or large format equipment you will have to rely on professional labs for your processing (or do your own), as the budget high-street and mail-order labs are set up only for 35mm. As digital photography becomes more widespread, digital backs for larger cameras are now available but these are very expensive and slow to 'save' images.

'Medium format' generally refers to cameras that use 120 or 220 film. Depending on the camera, this gives images that are 6x4.5cm, 6x6cm, 6x7cm or 6x9cm. While the Hasselblad is the most well-known medium format camera, its square (6x6) images will usually have to be cropped to suit the needs of magazine pages and for this reason many professionals choose the rectangular format offered by cameras such as the Mamiya RB67. Although most medium format cameras are true professional tools and offer a range of lenses and other accessories, the ultra-telephoto or super-wide lenses that are available for many 35mm systems are not manufactured for this format. Most cameras of this type allow interchangeable backs to be fitted, which means

⌃MGF, Penwyllt, Brecon Beacons, South Wales. Cambo 5x4 camera, 150mm lens, Fuji Velvia.

⌃Alfa Romeo 6C 1750, South Cerney, Gloucestershire. Mamiya RB67, 180mm lens, Fuji Velvia.

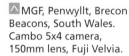

◁Jaguar E-type, near Calais, France. Canon EOS1n, 70–200mm lens, Fuji Provia.

▷This scene contained a great deal of fine detail and was likely to be used as the main picture in a magazine feature, so medium format was chosen to ensure that the final image was of the highest quality. The camera was set on a tripod before the cars were moved into place and, on a day when high winds were blowing the clouds quickly across the sky, I waited patiently until the sun started to break through, giving the dappled light on the distant hillside and the sparkle on the surface of the lake.
Austin-Healey 3000 Mk1 (foreground) and Austin-Healey Sprite Mk1, Loch Lomond, Scotland. Mamiya RB67, 65mm lens, Fuji Velvia.

◁These three pictures illustrate the different sizes of film employed by three different formats, and it is clear that if the same film type is used in each, the final image will require significantly less enlargement, for a given size, when larger film is used. However, in the case of both the 5x4in and 120 images, the circumstances allowed for the increased setting-up and shooting time involved, while for the 35mm shot of the Jaguar it was important to work quickly as the car was stationary on a busy road. An attempt to shoot on a larger camera may have resulted in a missed opportunity.

that the photographer can change from one type of film to another without using the entire roll. Many allow instant-film backs to be used, which is a huge bonus for the professional as it allows a final check on lighting, exposure and focus to be made before shooting any regular film.

'Large format' usually refers to cameras that use sheet film of 5x4 inches or even larger. Although not commonly used by photographers working for magazines, large formats are favoured by some advertising photographers and many who shoot cars in the studio use nothing else. Large format cameras have the additional benefit that they allow camera 'movements' –

the front and rear panels can be tilted, swung, or moved up and down. These movements allow distortion to be eliminated and depth-of field to be increased. Large format film comes in sheets, which have to be loaded into slides before use, but this has the advantage that each sheet can be shot and processed individually, allowing precise control. Instant-film backs are also available for cameras of this type.

Photographers used to using 35mm cameras will find that learning to use larger formats takes some while, but for the dedicated photographer – and the aspiring professional – the extra quality of the bigger images may well be worth the effort.

Why change lenses?

Why is the ability to change lenses so important to the car photographer? Action photography in particular is virtually impossible without a telephoto lens, which allows the photographer to fill the frame with the subject from a safe distance. Telephoto or zoom lenses are absolutely essential for almost any kind of motorsport photography, as safety rules at venues demand that spectators are kept at a considerable distance from the action. Wide-angle lenses are also useful tools and the creative car photographer will appreciate the flexibility that being able to change from one lens to another in seconds provides.

Most SLR cameras are sold complete with a

◁ At any motorsport event a telephoto lens is necessary to take pictures where the car is sufficiently large in the frame. To shoot this view at the distinctive Monaco Grand Prix circuit the photographer used a telephoto lens in combination with a teleconverter that further extends the focal length. **Ferrari F2001 at 2001 Monaco Grand Prix. Canon EOS1v, 200mm lens with 1.4x converter, Fuji Velvia.**

 Even when shooting on the road, a telephoto lens is essential to take this type of picture safely. The car was cornering at speed and a 300mm lens meant that I was able to shoot from the verge without having to worry. The other effect of using a telephoto lens is that the background is thrown well out-of-focus, making the car stand out; although this corner was carefully chosen for its relatively uncluttered background there is a length of 'Armco' visible.
Triumph TR5, near Wells, Somerset, England. Nikon F3, 300mm lens, Fuji Provia.

standard lens of around 50mm. This provides a field of view that is similar to that of the human eye, but you'll soon discover its limitations. Shoot at a race circuit and you'll need a magnifying glass to spot the cars on your finished picture. So for most keen car photographers, a telephoto lens will be the first essential accessory. Zoom lenses, which offer a range of focal lengths in one lens, are the most popular choice, and most manufacturers make an affordable lens with a focal length of around 70–200mm. The big advantage of a zoom lens is that the picture can be precisely framed without the photographer needing to change position, but against this must be balanced the fact that a 70–200mm lens will be heavier and more awkward to hand-hold than a lens with a fixed focal length of 200mm. It will also cost more.

Lenses longer than 200mm cost considerably more money, but the keen motorsport photographer may soon feel the need of a lens of 300mm or more. Many professionals specialising in this field own lenses of 400mm, 500mm or even

longer, but these are enormously expensive and a difficult purchase for even the keenest amateur to justify.

Fortunately, good quality wide-angle lenses can be bought for reasonable cost and these are a valuable addition to the car photographer's kit. They can be used to create dramatic car pictures on location but are particularly useful when shooting indoors at motor shows or museums, where it may not be possible to include an entire car in the frame when using a standard lens. Professional car photographers regularly use wide-angle lenses to shoot stunning action pictures, and to shoot car interiors.

While purists will wish to buy lenses from their camera's manufacturer, a cheaper alternative is to buy lenses from independent makers. These companies produce lenses in fittings to suit many different cameras and many of these are excellent value, but it pays to read the reviews in camera magazines where lenses are subjected to scientific scrutiny; cheap lenses can turn out to offer disappointing image quality.

 Wide-angle lenses can be used to create dramatic action pictures. Here the safe confines of a test track enabled a valuable and very rare car to be driven close enough to the back of the camera car for a 24mm lens to be used and this, combined with a shutter speed of 1/30th of a second, helped give the 'groundrush' effect in the foreground that conveys a feeling of speed. Autumn sunlight provided the attractive light on the trees lining the track.
Jaguar D-type, test track at Chobham, Surrey, England. Canon EOS1n, 24mm lens, Fuji Provia.

Perspective

One of the most important effects of using different lenses is the change in apparent perspective that this brings about. It's important to realise that perspective is controlled by the camera's viewpoint and not the lens itself; using a variety of lenses to shoot a car from the same viewpoint and cropping the finished pictures to make the car the same size in each would yield a set of almost identical images. But fitting different lenses and moving back and forth changes the *apparent* perspective. Wide-angle lenses seem to exaggerate perspective, making objects at different distances from the camera appear further apart, while telephoto lenses appear to compress the perspective, making distant objects seem closer together.

This is an important concept for the car photographer to understand, particularly when shooting static pictures. The relationship between a car and the landscape or background behind it can be completely altered by changing lenses. The best way to understand and appreci-

◁ This image was shot with a 65mm lens on the 6x7cm format, a moderately wide-angle lens. Notice how much of the distant scenery can be seen, and also that the front of the car appears to be 'stretched'. A wider lens would have exaggerated this effect still further, the end result being a picture that would have been unsuitable for most car magazines, as it would give a misleading impression of the car's true shape. Compare this picture to the one on the facing page to see the effect of changing to a longer lens.
Mercedes-Benz 190SL, Monaco. Mamiya RB67, 65mm lens, graduated grey filter, Fuji Velvia.

ate this is to park a car in an appropriate setting – such as in front of a building – and then fit varying lenses to your camera and examine the differences in composition. Start with a wide-angle lens and fill the width of the frame with the car; you will have a large amount of the building visible in the background. Then switch to a telephoto and move back so that the car again fills the width of the frame; you will now only have a narrow section of the building as background. This difference can be exploited by the creative photographer, especially to remove cluttered or distracting elements from the background of a car picture. By carefully positioning a car and then selecting the most appropriate lens you can make the most of any chosen setting.

There's another good reason why car photographers need to grasp the idea of perspective and lenses: the effect on the car itself. Repeat the exercise described above, but this time look carefully at the shape of the car when viewed through the different lenses. You will see that using a wide-angle lens exaggerates the length of the car, making it appear to have an excessively long front. This effect can be very unflattering to certain cars and is more pronounced with wider lenses. For this reason, it is best to avoid

shooting cars from close range with any lens of shorter focal length than 28mm (on 35mm cameras). Lenses wider than this will give the car an unnatural, almost distorted appearance.

Conversely, telephoto lenses will tend to give the impression of compressed perspective and this suits many cars, just as telephoto lenses are the best choice when shooting people. Many professional car photographers choose to use a short to medium telephoto lens (around 100mm or 135mm, or the medium format equivalents) for much of their static work, finding that this provides a pleasing perspective effect. Longer lenses will compress the perspective still further and this can produce some really striking images.

In each individual circumstance it is important to bear in mind the changes that can be made to your composition by changing lenses. It's well worth spending the time to try the various focal length lenses you have before settling on one choice, and shooting more than one option where time allows.

Standard lenses

Most 35mm SLR cameras come complete with a lens of around 50mm, and this is known as a standard lens. (For any film format, the focal length of the standard lens is approximately equivalent to the distance from corner to corner of the area of the film; for the 6x6cm format the standard lens is around 80mm and for 5x4in cameras it's around 150mm.) Some 35mm cameras are supplied with a short zoom lens of around 35–80mm as standard and many com-

◁ Many professional car photographers find that a lens of around 35mm or 50mm is the ideal choice for 'tracking' pictures – shooting one car from another. It allows the car to be driven at a reasonably safe distance while still making a dramatic picture. Here the camera was tilted slightly to produce a strong diagonal composition, and a shutter speed of 1/30th of a second provided the right amount of 'blur'. **Honda NSX, near Llangollen, North Wales. Canon EOS1n, 35mm lens, Fuji Velvia.**

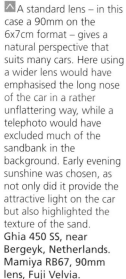
A standard lens – in this case a 90mm on the 6x7cm format – gives a natural perspective that suits many cars. Here using a wider lens would have emphasised the long nose of the car in a rather unflattering way, while a telephoto would have excluded much of the sandbank in the background. Early evening sunshine was chosen, as not only did it provide the attractive light on the car but also highlighted the texture of the sand. Ghia 450 SS, near Bergeyk, Netherlands. Mamiya RB67, 90mm lens, Fuji Velvia.

pact cameras have a fixed lens of around 38mm, so for that format we'll consider the term 'standard lens' to mean lenses of focal lengths from 35mm to 80mm.

Many professional photographers prefer a 35mm lens to the 50mm as a general all-round lens, preferring the slightly wider field of view. If you're buying a new camera the short zoom lens, of around 35–80mm, is well worth considering as an alternative to the fixed 50mm lens; many camera shops offer this option for a few extra pounds. Some of the more sophisticated compact cameras also come with a short zoom instead of a fixed lens.

Despite the usefulness of other lenses, the standard lens is a valuable tool that should not be disregarded. A 50mm lens has a field of view of around 45°, and this is similar to our field of vision. So photographs taken with these lenses have a natural-looking perspective, and this is an important factor in car photography.

Cars shot with wide-angle lenses can look unnaturally distorted, so the standard lens has

much to commend it, for static pictures in particular. The standard lens is also a relatively simple design to manufacture; the makers don't need to compromise the quality of the lens in order to produce a wide-angle or telephoto effect. This means that the quality of the images it provides is outstanding. Most standard lenses have wide maximum apertures, which means that focusing is easy and pictures can be taken in low light, and they weigh little, making it easier to hand-hold the camera. Many standard lenses also have the facility to focus closer than telephoto lenses, making it easier to take close-up shots.

In some circumstances there is an argument for taking just a standard or short zoom lens: if you're traipsing around, for example, an outdoor event such as a car show, carrying a bag full of gear is inconvenient and there will be few opportunities missed through lack of other lenses. Working with just one lens forces you to work harder on making the best possible picture; all too often swapping lenses is an attempt to try to make a dull picture more interesting.

There was limited space to work in here, and experimenting with various lenses showed that the 90mm standard lens created the most pleasing arrangement; if I used a wide-angle the more distant car was too small in the frame while there wasn't enough room to move back further with a telephoto. This was a busy square and I had to keep waiting until passers-by moved out of the frame, then shoot quickly. A warm-up filter was used to enhance the colours of the surrounding buildings on a dull winter's day. Maserati 3200 GT (on left) and Maserati 3500 GT, Mantova, Italy. Mamiya RB67, 90mm lens, 85B warm-up filter, Fuji Velvia.

Telephoto lenses

If there is one accessory that the keen car photographer really cannot do without, it is a telephoto lens. In much the same way as looking through binoculars or a telescope, this allows the photographer to fill the frame with a distant object, and the longer the focal length the greater the degree of magnification. Most action

photography needs such a lens if it is to be done safely and this is certainly the case when shooting motorsport. Most photographers now choose to purchase a zoom lens – this is a lens that offers a range of focal lengths, rather than just one. Nowadays these are available at reasonable cost and the image quality will be indistin-

◁ For 'panning' shots like this, on the road or at the race circuit, a telephoto lens of around 200mm is the ideal choice. It allows the photographer to stand at a reasonable distance and to follow the car in a smooth 'sweep' as it passes. A 70–200mm zoom lens is particularly useful for images like this as there isn't always enough space to move far enough back to use a fixed 200mm lens. This location was chosen for the trees alongside the road, which gave a good impression of speed as the camera panned with the car. A shutter speed of 1/60th of a second created the right amount of blur while keeping the car sharp. **Jaguar C-type, near Brescia, Italy. Nikon F3, 70–200mm lens, Fuji Provia.**

Motorsport pictures like this are impossible without a telephoto lens. A head-on shot was possible in complete safety from a viewpoint to one side of the car's intended route. With the rally car approaching the camera at speed, auto-focus was used to keep the image sharp while I concentrated on framing. Because the car's front had plenty of contrasting detail, and was in bright sunshine, the auto-focus coped well and the result was a sequence of sharp pictures. A shutter speed of 1/250sec was selected which is usually enough to 'freeze' a car when shooting from head-on.
Rover Metro 6R4, rallycross course near Silverstone, England. Canon EOS1n, 70–200mm lens, Fuji Provia.

guishable from that of a fixed focal length tele-photo. A good all-round zoom lens is a 70–200mm or similar, although motorsport photographers may find that for frame-filling action shots they need a lens of at least 300mm.

Telephoto and zoom lenses are larger and heavier than standard lenses, and this needs to be borne in mind when using them; the likelihood of 'camera shake' is greatly increased and, if the lens is being hand-held, a faster shutter speed will be necessary to counteract this. As a rule of thumb, it is usually possible to hand-hold a 50mm standard lens with a shutter speed of around 1/60th of a second. To be sure of hand-holding a tele-photo lens without incurring camera shake, you can do a rough conversion of focal length to a fraction of a second: so a 200mm lens will need 1/250th of a second, a 500mm will need 1/500th of a second. This is only a guide and in some circumstances – when shooting 'panning' action shots, for example – it's a rule that needs to be broken. At least one manufacturer now makes lenses that feature 'image stabilisation', technology which aims to help prevent camera shake.

Telephoto lenses also present a problem when it comes to depth-of-field. This is the amount of

the subject, in front of or behind the point of focus, which appears sharp on the final photo-graph. The smaller the aperture selected, the greater the depth of field but the longer the corresponding shutter speed needs to be. As tele-photo lenses give inherently less depth-of-field than their short focal length counterparts, and need faster shutter speeds – and therefore, wide apertures – this means that focusing must be extremely accurate. Long lenses in particular have extremely shallow depth of field and a moving car will pass through this narrow band of focus in a fraction of a second. This is often where auto-matic focusing comes into its own.

An additional accessory that may be worth considering is a teleconverter. This is an adaptor that goes between the camera body and the lens, and doubles the lens's focal length. So a 70–200mm zoom lens becomes a 140–400mm zoom. This is an inexpensive way of using very long focal length lenses, although image quality is compromised and the teleconverter absorbs two stops of light. But it can be useful in a situation such as a grand prix where spectators, and even accredited photographers, are kept a very long way back from the track for safety reasons.

Telephoto lenses are also useful for static images. Here the car was parked on the brow of a small hill, and I chose a viewpoint looking up at the car for maximum impact. I focused on the front of the car and the lens's narrow depth-of-field meant that the car stood out from the foreground and the background, which are both out-of-focus. Switching on headlamps can sometimes add interest to static pictures but these can look odd in bright sunlight, and there is always the danger of flattening the car's battery.
Lotus Elan +2, Clee Hill, Shropshire, England. Nikon F3, 300mm lens, Fuji Provia.

Wide-angle lenses

For the 35mm format, a wide-angle lens is one with a focal length shorter than around 35mm. These lenses are useful when shooting in a confined space, but can also be used to create eye-catching pictures in a range of situations. The most popular choices of wide-angle for 35mm cameras are 28mm or 24mm, and most manufacturers make lenses of both focal lengths with well-corrected optics that give images with minimal distortion. It is well worth spending the extra money to buy a really good quality wide-angle lens. This design is not especially easy to manufacture and cheap lenses are prone to distortion, which can result in unnatural-looking pictures. They can also suffer from poor sharpness at the extreme edges of the frame, particularly when used at wide apertures.

Wide-angle zoom lenses of around 24–35mm are a popular purchase but it is worth bearing in mind that these are far more complicated to manufacture than telephoto zooms and image quality may not be as good as with fixed focal length wide-angles. The zoom facility is not as useful on a wide-angle as on a telephoto. Zooms which include both wide-angle and telephoto extremes, such as 24–200mm lenses, are best

◁ Here I chose a wide-angle lens to create a dramatic driving shot. Using a waist-level viewfinder I was able to hold the camera just a few inches from the ground, which has provided the sense of speed on the tarmac. Both cars needed to be driven very close to the camera car (or they would have been too small in the frame) and this required good driving skills and a safe location with plenty of space. **Lamborghini Countach LP400 (on left) and Ferrari Berlinetta Boxer, airfield at Kemble, Gloucestershire, England. Nikon F3 with waist-level viewfinder, 24mm lens, Fuji Provia.**

care as the two cars have to be driven very close to each other. Shots of cars in groups are sometimes easier with a wide lens, especially where there is limited room. Where wide-angles really come in useful, though, is for shooting car interiors. These are inevitably tight spaces in which to work and a wide lens allows the photographer to include the whole interior.

The creative car photographer will soon learn to use a wide-angle lens to good effect and to avoid using it in situations where its false perspective can spoil the look of a beautiful car. As with so many things in photography, the best way to learn is to shoot lots of pictures, discard those that don't work and analyse the good ones carefully.

Although at first this seems a striking picture, it really serves as a good example of when not to use a wide-angle lens. This beautiful pre-war Alfa Romeo takes on the appearance of a weird hot rod with a long bonnet and huge flared front wings; a most unflattering image that bears no relation to the sleek curves of the car as seen 'in the flesh'.
Alfa Romeo 2900B, near Crickhowell, South Wales. Canon EOS1n, 24mm lens, Fuji Velvia.

Car interiors need a wide-angle lens. Here a 50mm lens was used on the 6x7cm format, equivalent to about a 24mm lens on 35mm. The camera was tripod mounted: light levels inside a car are always low, and here even using the last rays of the sun on a bright winter afternoon required an exposure of around ½ second as a small aperture was necessary to achieve sufficient depth-of-field.
Aston Martin Virage, Norfolk, England. Mamiya RB67, 50mm lens, Fuji Provia.

avoided as the compromise necessary in producing a lens of this design often means that image quality suffers.

Wide lenses give subjects like cars an exaggerated perspective and need to be used with care: in much the same way, a portrait shot with a wide-angle does the sitter no favours. However, wide-angles can also be used to create really striking pictures; shoot from low down and a car can be made to look really menacing. They also give greater depth-of-field, for a given aperture, than longer lenses. This means that by using a wide-angle lens and a small aperture you can shoot a car in a landscape setting and achieve sharpness that goes from the near point of the car to infinity.

Most keen car photographers will find wide-angle lenses particularly useful when working in indoor situations like museums or motor shows. Here, space is always at a premium and there are other factors to contend with, such as crowds or barrier fencing. Go in close to your subject with a wide lens and you can avoid such problems. Professional car photographers also use wide-angle lenses to take stunning action pictures when shooting from one car to another, but this approach needs skilled drivers and a great deal of

Unusual lenses

All the lenses described over the preceding pages are widely available, at reasonable cost. But in the case of both wide-angle and telephoto lenses there are extreme focal lengths that may be useful in certain circumstances. Such lenses are usually very expensive and even professional photographers may find it difficult to justify the outlay on a lens that will be used only occasionally, but one of the big advantages of the 35mm camera system is that manufacturers produce lenses for almost every circumstance.

Telephoto lenses longer than around 300mm are often referred to as 'ultra-telephotos'.

Manufacturers such as Canon and Nikon produce lenses of 400mm, 500mm, 600mm, 800mm and 1000mm as part of their comprehensive systems but these lenses are very expensive, heavy and unwieldy and are virtually impossible to hand-hold without incurring camera shake. Nevertheless, professional photographers who specialise in motorsport often have to rely on such lenses to get dramatic, frame-filling action shots. Modern motor racing is extremely safety-conscious, and over the years as speeds have increased so have the distances at which it is considered safe for photographers and spectators

◁ Ultra-telephoto lenses are essential for frame-filling action pictures at major motorsport events. Here the photographer selected a viewpoint with a clean, uncluttered background and shot each car as it came through. The band of sharp focus with lenses like this is only a few inches deep and considerable skill is needed to shoot sharp pictures. **Jordan EJ11 at 2001 German Grand Prix, Hockenheim, Germany. Canon EOS1v, 600mm lens, Fuji Velvia.**

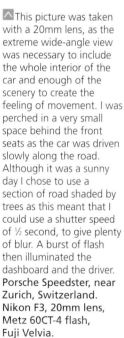

This picture was taken with a 20mm lens, as the extreme wide-angle view was necessary to include the whole interior of the car and enough of the scenery to create the feeling of movement. I was perched in a very small space behind the front seats as the car was driven slowly along the road. Although it was a sunny day I chose to use a section of road shaded by trees as this meant that I could use a shutter speed of ½ second, to give plenty of blur. A burst of flash then illuminated the dashboard and the driver. **Porsche Speedster, near Zurich, Switzerland. Nikon F3, 20mm lens, Metz 60CT-4 flash, Fuji Velvia.**

alike to watch the sport. At Grand Prix events in particular, the viewpoints available to even accredited professionals are a long way from the track and the only way round this is to fit an ultra-telephoto lens. If you're really serious about motorsport then a lens of 400mm or longer may turn out to be a wise investment but long lenses, with their very small depth-of-field, require considerable skill on the part of the photographer.

There are cheaper ways into the world of ultra-telephotos. The uses and limitations of tele-converters have already been described, but another option is the catadioptric or 'mirror' lens. This uses a sequence of mirrors to provide the image and the result is a very compact, light-weight lens of 500mm or longer. As ever, though, there's a downside; these lenses have a fixed aperture, usually around f/8, and this makes it very difficult to shoot action photography on all but the sunniest day without resorting to very fast film.

An ultra-wide-angle lens – 20mm or even shorter – is another accessory that it may be diffi-cult to justify buying but which is occasionally useful. Cheap examples are best avoided; a lens like this is complicated to manufacture and any compromise will result in a lens that gives poor

sharpness and a high degree of distortion. Professional car photographers will often use ultra-wide lenses to shoot in cramped car interi-ors but their exaggerated apparent perspective means that composition has to be carefully con-sidered. Extreme wide-angle or 'fish-eye' lenses are unlikely to be of much use to a car photogra-pher – in fact they are best avoided altogether as the gimmicky images they produce are a cliché that has definitely had its day.

There is a cheap way of obtaining access to exotic and expensive lenses, and that is to hire them as and when needed. Many professional dealers operate rental schemes and hold stocks of lenses like ultra-telephotos for the well-known camera systems. You'll usually have to pay a size-able, but returnable, deposit and if you want a particular lens for an event like a Grand Prix you'll need to book it well in advance, as other photo-graphers will undoubtedly have the same idea. This is also a good way of trying a piece of expensive equipment before purchasing, to make sure it's suited to your needs. And if you decide that you really need an ultra-telephoto or wide lens, it's worth keeping a close eye on classified ads and camera shops, as second-hand bargains do appear from time to time.

Lenses designed to focus on very small subjects are known as 'macro' lenses and although of limited value to the car photographer they can occasionally be useful for close-up details like this distinctive Porsche badge. Depth-of-field is very narrow in close-up photography and focusing needs to be done with care. The camera needs to be held with a steady hand, or tripod-mounted, as any slight movement will shift the point of focus. **Canon EOS1n, 50mm macro lens, Fuji Provia.**

Maximum aperture

Look through the catalogues of camera equipment suppliers and you will see that apparently similar lenses by the same manufacturer vary widely in price. The difference is in the lens's maximum aperture; that is, the size of the opening through which the light can pass to the shutter. (Lens apertures are measured in 'f stops'.) A 135mm lens with a maximum aperture of f/2 can cost three times as much as one with a maximum aperture of f/2.8, while a 300mm f/2.8 lens can

◁ Cornering shots on dull days need fast lenses; working from a safe distance means using a lens of 300mm or more and to create a sharp image this kind of photo needs a shutter speed of at least 1/250th of a second. Many professional photographers can justify the additional outlay involved in buying a fast lens, as they will use it often and most magazines prefer images shot on fine-grained film. This was taken on a particularly murky day and I was forced to uprate the film and 'push-process' it to gain an extra stop, even when using a 300mm f2.8 lens. **Lancia Delta Integrale, near Dolgellau, North Wales. Nikon F3, 300mm lens, Fuji Provia rated at ISO 200.**

Even when shooting on sunny days fast lenses are sometimes useful; here I wanted to 'freeze' the splash and this needed a shutter speed of 1/1000th of a second. Even in bright sunshine this meant shooting at f/2.8 on ISO 50 film. Several 'passes' were made, with the car hitting the water at a slightly different angle each time, to achieve the best result. Austin-Healey 100M, test track at Chobham, Surrey, England. Nikon F3, 300mm lens, Fuji Velvia.

cost five times as much as a 300mm f/4. Why should this be so, and can there really be a need to spend all that extra money for the sake of one additional stop?

The wider the maximum aperture of a lens, the larger the diameter of the front lens element needs to be. The difficulty arises because large front elements are more complicated – and expensive – to manufacture. A lens with a wide maximum aperture is said to be a 'fast' lens. Clearly, a wide aperture allows more light to pass than a narrow one. Correct exposure is achieved through a combination of shutter speed and aperture; choose a fast shutter speed and you will need to use a wide aperture to expose correctly. It therefore becomes clear why that extra stop can be so important to the photographer shooting action; on a dull day that additional stop can mean the difference between a sharp cornering shot and a blurred one or, worse still, no shot at all. Using a lens with a wide maximum aperture also enables professional photographers to use slower (that is, less sensitive) films, which have greater sharpness and better colour rendition – an important consideration when shooting

for magazines with good-quality reproduction.

It has to be said that most amateurs will find it hard to justify spending a great deal of money on a fast lens when the simpler option is to switch to more sensitive film in poor light. But fast lenses do have other benefits; most notably they provide a brighter viewfinder image (due to the extra light-gathering ability of the wider aperture). This makes focusing and composition much easier, particularly in very low light. For these reasons, many professional car photographers choose wide-angle and standard lenses with wide maximum apertures as well as fast telephotos.

The larger front elements of faster lenses are naturally more prone to fingerprints, dirt and scratches, and should be kept covered at all times when not in use. It is always good discipline to replace front and rear lens caps immediately after using a lens; damaged or smeared lenses are more prone to 'flare' and sharpness may suffer. Lenses should also be kept scrupulously clean, but use only proper lens-cleaning cloths. Handkerchiefs and pocket tissues are usually rather abrasive and sleeves are definitely not to be recommended!

Lenses with wide maximum apertures also make focusing easier in low light, and in the near-darkness outside this French hotel I needed to be able to focus accurately on this Jaguar. I used a flashgun to add some light to the rear of the car, while the light on the car's flanks is from another car, strategically positioned with its headlights on full beam. Jaguar E-type, near Calais, France. Canon EOS5, 24mm lens, Metz 60CT-4 flash, Fuji Provia.

Why use filters?

A filter is a piece of glass, or resin, that is fitted to the front of a lens to modify the light passing through it. There are many different types, from those intended to correct the colour balance of the light to so-called 'special effects' filters. The most useful types for the car photographer are graduated filters, polarising filters and colour-correction filters, but other types may occasionally come in useful. When it comes to choosing filters, there are two basic types: screw-on filters, made of glass and which screw on to the filter thread at the front of the lens; and filter 'systems', where an adaptor ring is attached to the thread and a filter holder is used to hold the filters. These are usually made of resin and are cheaper than glass filters. Some manufacturers also make thin gelatin filters that fit into filter holders.

Screw-on filters, such as those made by Hoya and B&W, offer the best optical quality, but there is the disadvantage that if the photographer owns a selection of lenses each may have a different diameter filter thread, creating a need to buy separate filters for each lens (although 'step-up' and 'step-down' adaptor rings can be bought to accommodate small differences in thread size). With the filter system, you need only buy one adaptor ring for each filter-thread size and the entire range of filters can then be used with every lens. Resin filters are prone to scratching and need to be handled and cleaned with care, but their modest cost means they can be

◁ 'Before' and 'after' photographs showing the effects of a warm-up filter, which was used to provide the more pleasing tone to the top picture. Shooting on a grey winter day I could tell that the light was very 'cold', tending to give a bluish tone to colour pictures. I chose to use quite a dense warm-up filter to provide the rich tones in the bank behind the car (which is actually a mound of salt outside a salt mine). Red, yellow or orange cars often benefit from the use of a warm-up filter, especially on overcast days.
Auburn Speedster, salt mine near Wilmslow, Cheshire, England. Mamiya RB67, 90mm lens, Cokin 85C warm-up filter, Fuji Provia.

The addition of a polarising filter (top) reduced the reflections on the bonnets of these three Austin-Healeys, improving the colour saturation and providing a much richer red to contrast with the bright yellow oilseed rape field in the background and the green grass.
Left to right: Austin-Healey 100M, Austin-Healey 3000, and Austin-Healey 4000, near Lichfield, Staffordshire, England. Mamiya RB67, 65mm lens, polarising filter, Fuji Velvia.

replaced regularly if damaged. The most popular filter system is that made by Cokin but many professional photographers choose the superior quality filters made by Hi-Tech or Lee Filters.

Filters are essential tools for creative photography, but before considering what they can do, it's important to realise what they can't do. No filter can turn a dull picture into a good one. There is a well-known phrase that states: 'if you're thinking of using filters, don't' and if you think your picture really needs a filter then the picture probably isn't worth taking. Filters should be used only to enhance an image, or to correct the colour balance of the light source, and shouldn't be seen as a last resort to improve a lifeless picture. In general, if it is clear from looking at a picture that a filter has been used, then that picture has failed.

Having made that clear, it's important for a photographer to recognise situations where a filter will improve a photograph; when a graduated filter will reduce the contrast between the foreground and a bright sky, when a polarising filter will remove an unwanted reflection or when a warm-up filter will provide a lift to pictures shot on a dull day. It's better to buy a small selection of carefully chosen filters than to buy a wide range, most of which will sit unused in the camera bag. And it's certainly important to avoid some of the more outlandish special effects filters. The best way of learning to use filters is to shoot plenty of photographs, with and without, and carefully compare the results.

Graduated and warm-up filters

The most useful filter in a car photographer's gadget bag is a neutral-density graduated filter (sometimes known as a graduated grey). This is clear at the bottom and dark at the top, with a gradual blend between the two, and it serves to balance the contrast between the foreground and a bright sky. If you expose correctly for your subject, it is very often the case that the sky above will appear too light on the finished picture, and a graduated grey filter solves this problem. Landscape photographers often use a graduated grey filter on nearly every picture they shoot, to preserve tone in the sky and to emphasise clouds.

These filters are made with different densities and it is well worth owning at least two types to cope with different situations; when shooting against the light, for example, it may be necessary to use a graduated filter that darkens the sky by as much as two stops but ordinarily this would result in a sky that appeared artificially dark on the final image. Although screw-on graduated filters are made, most photographers will choose those made for filter systems as they can be carefully positioned within the holder, depending on where the horizon falls in the frame. Care needs to be taken when shooting with a graduated filter at small apertures on wide-angle lenses, as

◁ The threatening sky in this picture was further enhanced by the addition of a graduated grey filter, and this had the effect of making the silver car stand out well from the background. The filter was carefully positioned to coincide with the horizon; had it been too far down in the filter holder it might have darkened the top of the car and made it look as though the paint on the roof was a different colour to that on the bonnet. **Mercedes-Benz 300 SLR, airfield near Stuttgart, Germany. Mamiya RB67, 65mm lens, graduated grey filter, Fuji Velvia.**

ing to their density: an 81C is significantly darker than an 81A and will produce a much more pronounced warm tone. It is worth remembering that if you use a digital camera with automatic white balance, this will simply counter the effect of the warm-up filter, so you will need to use an override facility if you have one. (It may be easier to add the warm tone later on the computer.) The same problem will apply if you use colour print film; the machines which print your films are set to produce a standard colour balance and if you've used a coloured filter the machine will simply counteract it at the printing stage. You can try telling the lab when you hand your films in that you're trying to achieve a particular effect, but don't rely on the information reaching the machine's operator.

⌄ Coloured graduated filters need to be used with care. Here I was able to get away with a tobacco grad because of the fact that the car was red and the background predominately brown; without some sort of graduated filter the sky would have appeared too light. I used an 85A as well as the graduated filter to create an overall warm tone.
Ferrari Dino 246 GT, Brecon Beacons, South Wales. Mamiya RB67, 180mm lens, 85A warm-up and tobacco graduated filters, Fuji Provia.

⌃ Shooting on a cloudy – and very cold – February day I chose to use a warm-up filter on this driving shot of an Alfa Spider, which has enhanced the red colour of the car and given a warm tone to the road and the background. The picture was for a spring edition of a magazine, and part of a supplement about driving sports cars; the uncorrected cold light would hardly have created an appropriate mood!
Alfa Romeo Spider, New Forest, Hampshire, England. Canon EOS1n, 35mm lens, 85B warm-up filter, Fuji Velvia.

the increased depth-of-field can result in the division between dark and light sections of the filter appearing as a visible line on the finished picture. Graduated filters are also made in colours other than grey, but these need to be used sparingly; while a brown or tobacco graduated filter can sometimes be used successfully, those that turn skies garish shades of pink or green should definitely be left at home.

Another valuable filter is the 'warm-up' filter. Colour film is balanced for average daylight but every day is different. Often a dull winter's day can result in pictures that have a distinctly bluish hue, and shooting in the shade on a sunny day can present the same problem. Warm-up filters, which have a distinct brown or orange tone, can counteract this, and in any case pictures with a warmer tone are somehow more pleasing to the eye. This is especially the case when photographing people as the warm tone imparts a healthier colour to skin, but look carefully at car advertisements and you will notice how many are shot using warm-up filters to create a pleasing mood.

Warm-up filters are usually labelled as 81 or 85 series filters and designated A, B or C accord-

Polarising, neutral density and colour correction filters

Light travels in many different planes. A polarising filter eliminates light travelling in a particular direction and this has the effect of reducing reflections and improving colour saturation, an effect that works particularly well on cars. The filter rotates and has to be carefully adjusted to find the position where the effect is most pronounced. A polariser works well on blue skies, darkening the colour and producing a rich blue, but it is also useful on overcast days. One disadvantage is that the filter absorbs around one-and-a-half stops of light, which in poor light may force the photographer to use a tripod. Some cameras' auto-focus systems won't work with the 'linear' type of polarising filter and you may need to purchase the more expensive 'circular'

To create the blurred effect in the background on this shot I needed a total of six stops' worth of neutral density filters. I set the camera up while the ferry was still at the dock, double-checked the focus and then placed the filter over the lens and waited for the ferry to move, then shot a sequence of exposures of varying lengths as the ferry moved across the harbour. The exposure was around eight seconds, and I had to hope that the vibrations from the ferry's engine wouldn't affect the camera.
Porsche Speedster, ferry at Balboa Island, south of Los Angeles, California, USA. Canon EOS1n, 24mm lens, 2 x 3-stop neutral density filters, Fuji Velvia.

such as a polariser, can be used to achieve the same result.

In some situations, particularly when shooting indoors or under artificial light sources, colour film will take on an unsightly colour cast. This is where colour correction filters come in; fluorescent lighting in particular imparts an ugly green cast on colour film and this needs to be corrected. A CC (colour correction) filter called a CC30M (for magenta) will remove this and give neutral tones, as will a specially made correction filter called an FL-D, (for so-called 'daylight' tubes) or an FL-W (for 'white' tubes). Tungsten lights will create an orange cast that can be corrected with an 80B (for blue) filter. Many professional photographers own a colour temperature meter, which effectively tests the colour of the light source and suggests which CC filters are needed to create neutral tones on colour film, but this is only really necessary for work where colour matching is critical. Digital cameras that have automatic white balancing will make allowance for the colour of the light source, removing the need for colour correction filters, and if you shoot on colour print film the lab's printing machine will do the same.

▽Here, working under fluorescent lights, a CC30M filter gave a neutral rendition; although I could have used flash it would have been impossible to light all three cars evenly with just one flashgun, and the fluorescent lights would still have caused the green cast to be visible in the background. The filter absorbs around one stop of light but since a tripod is essential in indoor situations this isn't a problem.
Maserati Indy, Maserati Ghibli and Maserati Merak, museum at Bassano del Grappa, Italy. Canon EOS1n, 24mm lens, CC30M filter, Fuji Provia.

△Although many photographers will be familiar with the effect of a polarising filter on blue skies, it can be equally useful in overcast conditions. Here it served to reduce the reflection on the bonnet of the car, making the bright red stand out from the background.
Ferrari 275GTB/4, near Nassau, Bahamas. Mamiya RB67, 90mm lens, polarising filter, Fuji Provia.

type – check your camera's instruction manual for details. One word of warning: some laminated car windscreens display an odd pattern when viewed through a polarising filter and this can spoil an otherwise good photograph – look carefully for this when adjusting the filter.

Neutral density (ND) filters simply reduce the amount of light passing through the lens without modifying it in any other way. At first this might seem a slightly odd thing to want a filter to do, but there are numerous situations when, on a bright day, you may wish to use a slow shutter speed or a wide aperture to create a particular effect and even with slow film there's still too much light. ND filters are made in one-stop, two-stop and three-stop densities but can of course be used in combination to achieve the desired reduction in light. Once you've fitted an ND filter it can be difficult to compose and focus carefully so it may be best to put the filter on after you've decided on your viewpoint and set the focus. If you don't own an ND filter then other filters,

Other filters

There are some other filters that may come in useful from time to time. Some photographers choose to leave an ultra-violet (UV) filter, sometimes known as a skylight filter, on their lens at all times. This filter is supposed to remove some of the ultra-violet from daylight and thereby reduce haze, but its effect is minimal and it really serves as lens protection. There is really little point in spending money on an expensive lens and then compromising its optical quality by leaving a filter on it at all times, but against this must be balanced the fact that it is much cheaper to replace a scratched filter than a scratched lens. If you really feel that protecting the lens in this way is important, buy a good quality UV filter and keep it scrupulously clean.

To create an 'impressionist' feel to this picture I used a soft-focus filter. The location suited this approach and the filter has had the effect of muting the colours, giving a tranquil mood to the picture. The girl and the waiter were friends of the writer who'd arranged the shoot, and the table and chairs were props borrowed for the occasion. When using a soft-focus filter the degree of softness will be controlled in part by the lens aperture; small apertures will lessen the effect of the diffusion.
Ford Vedettes, Poudenas, Lot et Garonne, France. Mamiya RB67, 65mm lens, soft focus filter, Fuji Velvia.

△A strong red filter used here had the effect of darkening the blue sky, as well as making the car and the stone of the building stand out. I could have darkened the sky by burning it in at the printing stage but it would have been tricky to do this accurately around the outline of the building.
Volvo 262C, near Llangollen, North Wales. Canon EOS1n, 24mm lens, red filter, Kodak CT400N.

A filter called a 'sunset' filter is a sort of hybrid graduated filter and warm-up, with a darker orange colour at the top, that is to supposed to create the effect of shooting at sunset. Used with care it can sometimes provide the desired effect, in particular if actually shooting at that time of day but in circumstances where the colours are rather muted. Beware of over-using filters like this.

If you don't own a macro lens, then close-up filters can be useful for shooting details. These are available in differing strengths that focus at different distances. A soft focus, or diffuser, filter can occasionally be used to create a mood; it diffuses colours and softens hard edges and often works well shooting against the light. Used with fast film it enhances grain, which can sometimes create unusual and striking images. Sometimes when shooting at night a 'starburst' filter can be used to create a star effect around point sources of light, but these also tend to soften the image and the same effect can be achieved by stopping the lens down.

When it comes to shooting in black-and-white, it may seem surprising that colour filters are useful. But use a strong red filter and it will have the effect of lightening reds and darkening blues and greens in the scene; so a red car will stand out against a dark blue sky. Use a green filter and a red car will appear darker while grass and foliage will stand out. Yellow or orange filters can also be used to darken skies and make white clouds stand out. If you're a regular user of black-and-white it's well worth owning the full set of coloured filters as they can be used to control the levels of contrast in your finished picture depending on which colours are prevalent.

Some manufacturers, aiming at the amateur market, produce a range of filters known as 'special effects' filters. They include multi-image prisms, 'speed' filters that supposedly create an impression of movement, and filters that will put an artificial rainbow across the top of your picture or that surround a central clear section with a soft-focus purple colour. Needless to say, these are gimmicky effects that are never successful and have no place in the creative photographer's equipment. Spend the money instead on some more film and concentrate on developing your own ideas.

△Sometimes using filters in an unconventional manner can produce worthwhile results; here as well as using a graduated grey filter on the sky I used another, the other way up in the filter holder, to darken the foreground. This has the effect of leading the eye into the picture and making the car stand out.
Ferrari 400i, near Royston, Hertfordshire, England. Mamiya RB67, 65mm lens, two graduated grey filters, Fuji Provia.

Tripods

For static car photography, a tripod is an essential piece of equipment. You will rarely see a professional photographer working without one. The most obvious benefit is the elimination of camera shake; a tripod allows any shutter speed to be chosen without the risk of the picture being spoiled by any slight movement as the shutter is released. (SLR cameras are particularly prone to camera shake, as the act of pressing the shutter button first flips the camera's mirror out of the way.)

But there are other good reasons for using a tripod, most notably for the working method it imposes on the photographer. In low-light situations it is rarely possible to hand-hold a camera without resorting to fast films. Put the camera on a tripod and you can choose to use slower films, with their inherently superior quality.

Additionally, remember that the depth-of-field in a photograph is largely dependent on the lens aperture selected; small apertures give greater depth-of-field but need correspondingly longer shutter speeds. With your camera

Shooting at this time of day a tripod is essential; light levels are low and even using fast film a wide aperture would be necessary. With the camera tripod-mounted I could use ISO 50 film, which is much better at handling the subtle colours in a scene like this than faster film would be. I was also able to use an aperture of f/16, which ensured that the car and the aeroplane were both sharp.
Lago Record, airfield near High Wycombe, Buckinghamshire, England. Mamiya RB67, 65mm lens, Fuji Velvia.

When creating a picture like this, where cars have to be carefully positioned and the camera placed in an exact position to make the most of the various elements within the scene, a tripod allows the photographer to concentrate fully on the composition. The stone wall and yellow tree, found in an Oxfordshire village, provided the ideal setting for two quintessentially British cars. **MGA (in foreground) and MG TF, near Oxford, England. Mamiya RB67, 180mm lens, Fuji Velvia.**

securely on a tripod, you can select the desired aperture without having to worry about the length of the shutter speed this imposes. Remember also that telephoto lenses are more difficult to hand-hold than standard or wide-angle lenses, and very often have a threaded socket to enable them to be tripod-mounted. (You should always use this in preference to the thread on the base of the camera, as the whole set-up will be better balanced.) And virtually all medium- and large-format cameras need to be used on a tripod, being almost impossible to hand-hold successfully.

As well as the technical advantages of using a tripod, there is a more esoteric reason for doing so. With a camera in a fixed position, you can concentrate more fully on the viewfinder image. This results in better composition and, ultimately, more successful pictures. Using a camera hand-held, it is all too easy to move from one viewpoint to another and shoot lots of film; put the camera on a tripod and you work that much harder to create your intended result before releasing the shutter. You will soon find that, when using a tripod, you tend to check

the corners of the frame more carefully, and you will spot distracting elements in a scene more readily. And if you're shooting a sequence of pictures of the same scene – such as when 'bracketing' exposures, for example – every shot will be taken from an identical viewpoint. This is much more difficult to do when hand-holding the camera.

When it comes to buying a tripod, it is essential to choose a sturdy one; a flimsy tripod is worse than none at all. Unfortunately the only really sturdy tripods are relatively big and heavy. To landscape photographers, who often have to carry their gear a long way, this is a major difficulty, but for car photographers it's much less of a problem. Wherever possible, you should avoid using a tripod at its fullest extension as this reduces its stability – this is certainly the case when the centre column is racked right up.

A tripod is of little use when shooting action photography, due to the need to follow the subject closely through the viewfinder, but a monopod can be extremely useful to reduce the possibility of camera shake, particularly when using very long lenses.

The period just after sunset can be one of the most rewarding for a car photographer, and a tripod is essential. The soft light and reflection of the sky have accentuated the distinctive curves of the two Porsches. To keep both cars sharp I shot at f/16 but there was so little light left in the sky that this dictated a shutter speed of 30 seconds; you can see how the clouds have blurred as they were blown across the sky during the exposure. **Porsche 911 (in foreground) and 356, near Banbury, Oxfordshire, England. Mamiya RB67, 65mm lens, graduated grey filter, Fuji Velvia.**

Flash 1

A flashgun is an important addition to the car photographer's equipment, and not just for shooting in indoor situations. There are numerous occasions on which using flash can liven up a photograph, both on dull days and on sunnier days when often a burst of 'fill-in' flash can relieve harsh shadows. To get the most out of flash you will need to be well versed not only in what it can do but in its limitations and like so many other photographic skills, using flash is one that needs plenty of practice to get right.

The first point to make is that the small flashguns that fit on to a camera's hot shoe are next to useless for car photography. A car is a large object to light and a small flash just isn't up to the job. Most professional photogra-

Dark cars shot on dull days often benefit from the addition of flash. To light this shot I used two flashguns: one provided the light on the front of the car and was positioned out of shot to the right of the camera, while the other, more powerful one was positioned to the left of the camera and created the highlights on the wheels. A long lead connected the smaller flash to the camera and a slave unit triggered the other. This is the kind of shot where automatic exposure or through-the-lens flash metering would be of no use whatsoever. I had to carefully judge the exposure to balance the flash and the available light, and selected a shutter speed to give exactly the right amount of tone in the sky. I then used instant film to check on the exposure.
Bugatti Type 50, near Watlington, Oxfordshire, England. Mamiya RB67, 90mm lens, Metz 60CT-4 and 45CT-5 flashguns, slave unit, Fuji Velvia.

As darkness crept in I added a burst of flash to liven up this shot. The flash was hidden behind the snow bank to the car's left and was attached to a slave unit; this was triggered by a small flash connected to the camera, but pointed at the ground so that the light from it didn't affect the shot. This was for a feature about driving a Caterham from the UK to the French Alps for a skiing trip.
Caterham 7, near Val d'Isère, France. Canon EOS1n, 24mm lens, 85B warm-up filter, Metz 60CT-4 flash, Fuji Velvia.

phers, and not just those who specialise in cars, buy the much bigger and heavier but more powerful 'hammer-head' type of flashgun, which has a separate battery pack. These are rechargeable, which gives the additional advantage that you don't need to keep buying replacement batteries, and a single charge will usually provide the pack with enough power for many flashes.

Another disadvantage of the hot-shoe-mounted flashgun is that, from a creative point of view, this is just about the worst position for a light source. Move the flash away from the camera, even at arm's length, and the light it provides is much better. For this you will need an extension lead and this exposes one of the weak links; the standard PC connection for triggering a flash that isn't on a hot shoe is notoriously unreliable. It is always worth keeping a spare flash-to-camera lead as these are flimsy and easily damaged, and long extension leads are also prone to a frustrating lack of reliability.

Many professional car photographers regularly use two or more flashguns at the same time, and

for this a 'slave unit' is necessary; this is a small sensor that triggers a flashgun when it detects another burst of flash. This all happens at the speed of light so all the flashes effectively fire simultaneously. Using a small flash close to the camera to trigger a (more powerful) slaved remote flash can be a more successful way of working than using long extension leads.

Modern flashguns are made to work in conjunction with cameras' sophisticated metering systems, and offer TTL (through-the-lens) metering to ensure accurate exposure. With the flash moved away from the camera this is less reliable, and in any case flash is often required to act as fill-in rather than as a main light source. This is where it becomes vital to know and understand your equipment, as correct exposure is far more likely if you are able to determine the camera and flash settings for yourself. Remember too that, with most cameras, flash cannot be used with faster shutter speeds; the second curtain of a focal plane shutter moves across the film just after the first and this usually restricts flash use to shutter speeds of 1/125 of a second or longer.

Using flash here enabled me to exploit the creative potential of the glorious sunset but still retain all the detail in the car's interior. I set an aperture on the lens of f/8 but then set the exposure dial on the flash to f/4 – this was to take account of the fact that, because the interior was predominantly dark, it could easily have been over-exposed by the flash. It was then a case of choosing a shutter speed that gave a correct exposure for the sunset. To be sure of a successful end result I then took several shots using different shutter speeds and different flash settings, but it was important to work quickly before the sun disappeared.
Ferrari 330P, San Marino. Mamiya RB67, 50mm lens, Metz 60CT-4 flash, Fuji Velvia.

Flash 2

The key to using flash creatively is to appreciate the relationship between shutter speed, aperture and the flash exposure. We already know that a correct exposure is achieved by balancing shutter speed and aperture and if we add a burst of flash into the equation we have another variable that will affect the finished picture. Here's the important point: while the aperture setting on the lens will affect the flash exposure, the shutter speed makes no difference to it at all. (This is because the flash duration is typically 1/1000th of a second or shorter.) The creative car photographer can exploit this fact to good effect, both for action shots and striking static pictures.

Here's an example of how this works. Let's assume you're taking a static shot of a car on a dull day, but adding flash to improve the picture. The correct exposure, using the daylight alone,

◁ Here I wanted to create an action picture with lots of movement but also to retain sufficient detail in the car. The test track we were using had wooded sections and open sections that called for constant changes in the exposure, so I set the camera to 'aperture-priority' mode and chose an aperture of f/8, leaving the camera to adjust the shutter speed accordingly. I then set my flashgun to f/5.6 so that it would act as fill-in rather than as the primary light source. As we travelled through the darker sections of the track, the camera set long shutter speeds but the flash kept the car sharp enough. My guess is that the shutter speed here was around 1/8th of a second, giving the blurred background that creates the impression of speed.
Ferrari 375MM, test track near Chobham, Surrey, England. Canon EOS1n, 24mm lens, Metz 60CT-4 flash, Fuji Provia.

⌃This is another example where flash was used to fill-in detail, rather than as a main light source. I chose a long shutter speed to create the feeling of movement, and set the flashgun at one stop less than the aperture on the lens. Without flash the interior and dashboard of the car would have appeared too dark, and the burst of flash has served to keep the dials and other details sharp. The driver chose his outfit to suit the car; modern clothing would have looked completely out of place in a vintage Bentley.
Bentley Speed Six, lane near Watlington, Oxfordshire, England. Canon EOS 1n, 20mm lens, Metz 60CT-4 flash, Fuji Velvia.

would be 1/30th of a second at f/5.6. If you set the flashgun to f/5.6, the front of the car will be correctly exposed. But if you set the shutter speed to 1/60th of a second, or 1/125th of a second (leaving the aperture and the flash set to f/5.6) the front of the car will still be correctly exposed while the background will be underexposed. This can be used to make a car stand out from a distracting background or to emphasise a moody sky. This is a technique that needs considerable practice and trial-and-error experimentation to become thoroughly familiar with, but is worth pursuing.

Action pictures can also be vastly improved by adding flash. A burst of flash will 'freeze' a moving car but if you select your shutter speed carefully you can produce stunning pictures of a pin-sharp car against a blurred background. An example: imagine you are shooting a car on a section of road surrounded by trees, which are blocking much of the daylight. The correct exposure, using just the available light, would be 1/30th of a second at f/2.8. If we stop the lens down two stops to f/5.6 we would need to

change the shutter speed to 1/8th of a second, but this would be too long an exposure to create a sharp image of a moving car. However, if we now add a burst of flash with the flashgun set to f/5.6, this will 'freeze' the car while the 1/8th of a second shutter speed will blur the trees in the background. Again, plenty of experimentation will be needed to ensure successful results but this is a recipe for really exciting action shots. Try using different shutter speed, aperture and flash settings, and analyse your results carefully to see which works best.

The important thing to understand about both of the above examples is that the light from a flashgun has only a short range, so while it will illuminate the car in both cases it won't reach the background. It's very important to discover and appreciate your flashgun's limitations, as expecting it to light a larger area than it has the power to do is a common cause of failed pictures. Many professional photographers own exposure meters that have a facility for measuring flash and this is a useful accessory, which can help to ensure correct exposure.

⌃Shooting from this angle with a 24mm lens and a shutter speed of 1/30th of a second, the car in the foreground would have been much too blurred. The flash has retained detail in the wheels and the front of the car yet there is still enough movement to create an impression of speed. Notice that the flash hasn't reached the second car or the background.
MGC (in foreground) and MGB GT, sprint course at Curborough, Lichfield, England. Canon EOS1n, 24mm lens, Metz 60CT-4 flash, Fuji Provia.

Other accessories

There are various other accessories that may come in handy. The most important is some form of specially designed camera case or bag, that allows gear to be carried comfortably and keeps dust, mud and rain away from your precious cameras and lenses. This should be of the type that allows each piece of equipment to be kept in its own partition, keeping it protected and ensuring it is readily found when needed.

Many professional photographers choose to measure exposure with a separate meter, rather than trusting that built-in to the camera. Most of these measure the light falling on a subject rather than the light reflected from it (as the camera

This is exactly the sort of picture where a camera's meter might struggle to expose correctly but where a separate hand-held meter allows for an exact reading to be taken. However, it's very important to have an understanding of how to judge the exposure in tricky situations like this. Shooting against the light always needs careful exposure metering and, if time allows, take several pictures at different settings. **Ford Comete Monte Carlo, near Reims, France. Mamiya RB67, 90mm lens, Fuji Provia.**

A motor drive is absolutely essential when shooting action pictures. Most professional quality cameras have a built-in motor drive that allows for shooting at up to six frames per second, more than enough to cope with a car passing at speed. **Porsche Speedster on race circuit near Nassau, Bahamas. Nikon F3, 70–200mm lens, Fuji Provia.**

does). This is particularly important in car photography, since a predominantly light or dark car can fool a camera's meter and lead to under- or over-exposure. Some photographers choose a 'spot meter', which measures the light from a very small part of the subject; this allows the user to base the exposure on the exact part of the subject they wish to be accurately exposed.

A lens hood, that fits on the front of the lens and prevents stray light from entering the lens, is an essential accessory that prevents lens flare from degrading image quality. It should be used at all times but it is important to ensure that the lens hood is designed to match the lens: if you use too long a lens hood on a wide-angle lens it will appear in the corners of the final image.

There are often occasions when a reflector of some kind proves useful. This can be nothing more complicated than a piece of white card, but this is awkward to carry around and you may prefer to invest in a specially made reflector that folds neatly into a bag.

When using a tripod, it is important also to use a cable release. This allows the shutter to be triggered without the risk of vibration. Many

modern cameras allow for the use of an electronic remote release that does the same job, but these tend to be rather more costly than the traditional mechanical type.

Most modern cameras have a built-in motor drive to wind the film on between each frame. However, many older SLRs lack this feature and if you wish to shoot action pictures a motor drive will be an essential purchase. Some manufacturers of modern SLRs make a 'booster pack' that increases the speed of the camera's built-in motor drive; this will be a worthwhile purchase for anyone who chooses to specialise in motor-sport or action photography. Check your camera manufacturer's catalogue to see the options that are available.

No photographer should go out without a specially designed lens cleaning cloth, and a blower brush is useful not only for removing dust from lenses but for keeping the inside of the camera free of stray particles that might scratch the surface of the film. While not strictly a photographic accessory, you will be surprised how often a Swiss Army knife or similar tool will come in handy when shooting on location.

To shoot this car interior on a sunny summer's day I moved it into the shade and used a reflector to bounce light back into the car. This reflector was of the type that is white on one side and gold on the other and I used the gold side, which has resulted in the picture having an overall warm tone. **AC Aceca, near Sunningdale, Berkshire, England. Canon EOS1n, 24mm lens, Fuji Velvia.**

Choosing film

Before deciding which type of film to choose it's important to consider what you actually want to do with your finished pictures. If you like to have prints to stick in an album or pass around then print film is the obvious choice, but if you are aiming to get your work published you will need to shoot on transparency (slide) film, as this is what magazine and book publishers require. If you are after superb quality images then transparency film will again be the best choice, since it provides superior sharpness and colour rendition when compared with print films. It's also worth

◁ A scene like this, that contains lots of fine detail and vivid colours, really needs the best quality film to do it justice. ISO 50 film has outstanding sharpness, very fine grain and good colour saturation. Its relative lack of sensitivity means that you are often forced to use a tripod but for images like this the careful photographer will use one as a matter of course. **Duesenberg Model J/SJ, southern Los Angeles, California. Mamiya RB67, 180mm lens, Fuji Velvia.**

Panning shots usually need shutter speeds of around 1/60th of a second and, even on an overcast day, ISO 50 film can be used. Depth-of-field is limited when using telephoto lenses so using wide apertures is not a disadvantage.
MGA near Malvern, Worcestershire, England. Canon EOS1n, 70–200mm zoom lens, Fuji Velvia.

remembering that if you shoot on print film the quality of the finished print will depend ultimately on the machine that processes and prints your work rather than on your input at the taking stage. This can be very frustrating and unless you have your own darkroom facilities you may find that you can achieve better quality by shooting on a digital camera and using an inkjet printer to make your prints. But don't be afraid to reject the work of a processing lab if you feel they haven't done your work justice; their machines are set to produce a reliable 'average' print and they will often agree to reprint any pictures you feel they have printed badly.

It's tempting to think that, for action photography in particular, fast (sensitive) film is necessary. This isn't the case; most of the time when shooting action you are attempting to create a feeling of movement and this often means using shutter speeds of 1/60th or 1/30th of a second, and slower film will easily cope with this. You should always aim to use films of around ISO 100 or slower wherever possible; even with the huge advances in film technology faster films inevitably display more grain and poorer colour rendition

than slower ones. Most professional photographers – who usually work with transparency materials – will use films like Fuji Velvia (ISO 50) or Provia (ISO 100) as standard and will only turn to faster films when poor light makes it necessary.

Always buy film from camera shops, and ideally from those that have a reasonably fast turnover. Film deteriorates over time, especially if not kept refrigerated, and it's best to avoid buying a roll that has been sitting on a shop shelf for a year. Keep film in the fridge, or even the freezer, until you want to use it, and avoid leaving film in the car on hot days. All of these precautions are even more important when buying professional materials, as these are intended to be bought and processed quickly. Films for the amateur market tend to be more resilient to abuse.

When you have found a film that you particularly like, it is well worth sticking with it. The more you use a film the more you become accustomed to its individual characteristics; you will be able to recognise circumstances when the film is likely to take on a colour cast or need an extra half-stop of exposure.

When shooting in unusual circumstances it is important to use a film that you are familiar with, so that you can anticipate how it will react to coloured lighting or long exposures. For this shot of a Jaguar in London's Soho it was important to work quickly as the car was parked in a restricted zone; I used a ten-second exposure and a burst of flash helped to light the front of the car.
Jaguar Mk X/420G, Soho, London, England. Mamiya RB67, 65mm lens, Metz 60CT-4 flash, Fuji Provia.

Black-and-white film

Far from being a relic of the days before colour film, black-and-white (or 'monochrome') film is as popular as ever. Many creative photographers actually prefer to use it, finding that, without the distraction of colour, they can produce graphic and dramatic images. Glossy magazines often illustrate entire features with monochrome images and there are numerous calendars and posters produced in black-and-white.

For the car photographer, it is always worth having a few rolls of black-and-white film in the camera bag, and to recognise circumstances when a monochrome image might be more appropriate than a colour one. Cars with a distinctive shape can often stand out more on a monochrome image than on a colour one. Black-and-white film can also be a valuable tool on really grey, overcast days when colour pictures may end up looking rather lifeless. On such days, high-speed mono films can provide an opportunity to create some really punchy, grainy images.

Monochrome films are no longer the preserve of those who have access to darkroom facilities. Films like Ilford XP2 or Kodak CT400N are 'chro-

▷ My intention here was to create a stark image in which the car would stand out from its surroundings. I uprated ISO 400 film to ISO 800, which had the effect of increasing the contrast, and fitted a red filter which darkened the vegetation. A shutter speed of one second made the falling water appear blurred and in the darkroom I burned in the sky, which would otherwise have been a distraction.
Opel Manta GTE, near Brecon, South Wales. Mamiya RB67, 90mm lens, red filter, Kodak T-Max 400 rated at ISO 800.

◁ A dull day and a rather uninspiring test track was not an ideal combination with which to produce striking images of the McLaren F1, so I chose to use black-and-white film. The soft light has helped to accentuate the car's distinctive lines, and in the darkroom I made the car stand out from its surroundings by 'burning-in' (darkening) the tarmac, the trees and the sky in the top right-hand corner.
McLaren F1, test track near Chobham, Surrey, England. Nikon F3, 35mm lens, Kodak T-Max 400.

For real enthusiasts, though, there is no substitute for the creative control and undoubted satisfaction that comes from making black-and-white prints in the traditional way. And no matter how good your inkjet printer, the quality of prints produced digitally doesn't approach that of those that emerge fresh from a tray of fixer. At least half of the creative input to a black-and-white image comes at the printing stage, whether done on a computer or an enlarger, and the committed photographer will want to acquire the skills of 'dodging' and 'burning-in' as well as understanding the uses of different grades of paper and techniques like toning or lith printing.

Being able to take successful black-and-white images depends on an ability to 'see' in monochrome, to visualise how the end result will look when viewing a potential subject in full colour. It's important to realise that apparently contrasting colours may be identical tones on a black-and-white print. Light that might produce glorious colour images – such as that early in the day or late in the evening – may actually give rather disappointing monochrome images. Once you've shot a few rolls, you'll readily recognise situations when black-and-white film might be the key to a really powerful image and those when it might be best to stick with colour.

∨ Modern monochrome films produce very fine-grain images, and if you really want chunky grain to create a mood you have to work at it. Here I used a Kodak film that can be rated at ISO 3200 or faster and while this gave a noticeable grain pattern I had to emphasise this still further by printing on high-contrast paper. **BMW M3, near Dungeness, Kent, England. Nikon F3, 300mm lens, Kodak T-Max 3200 film.**

mogenic' films that are compatible with the C-41 process that every high-street processing lab uses to process colour print films. This means that you can get your films processed quickly and easily without the need to spend hours in a darkroom handling mysterious chemicals, and these films – even the ISO 400 varieties – produce images with extremely fine grain. With the increased availability of low-cost, good quality scanners many photographers have dispensed with the traditional darkroom and now use computers and inkjet printers to produce their black-and-white prints.

Specialist films

It's useful to be aware of some of the different films that are available, some of which can offer exciting creative possibilities and some of which can provide solutions to technical problems. Most are readily available from good camera shops and can be developed by most processing laboratories.

Fast films – those of ISO 400 or more – are not only useful when shooting in poor light but the more pronounced grain they exhibit can be exploited to make interesting images. The problem is that modern films are designed to be fine-grained and achieving grainy images requires some effort. Choose the very fastest film you can find (some manufacturers make films designed to be used at ISO 1000 or more) and, in the case of transparency or regular black-and-white film, 'uprate' it; this means setting a higher ISO setting and then asking your lab to push-process the film accordingly. (Unfortunately this doesn't really work with colour print films or 'chromogenic' mono films.) The more a film is push-processed the grainier it will be but the colour rendition and the density of the blacks will suffer so film can't be pushed indefinitely. Using a diffuser (soft focus) filter will emphasise the grain and you could then choose to enlarge a small section of the final image to increase the grain still more.

Colour infra-red films give wildly unrealistic colours which, while not to everyone's taste, certainly make for unusual images. The different results here come from using two different filters; the cool blue image was shot using a yellow filter, while a red filter produced the garish yellow. Trial-and-error is the only way to learn to use these materials. Ford Edsel Ranger, near Petersfield, Hampshire, England. Nikon FE, 24mm lens, red/yellow filters, Kodak colour infra-red film.

For this picture I wanted really noticeable grain, so I chose film that could be rated at ISO 1600 and push-processed. Compare the picture below with the picture on the left, which was shot on ISO 100 film, and you will see that the contrast, and the density of the blacks, are much reduced on the fast film image. Maserati Ghibli Cup, near Halstead, Essex, England. Canon EOS1n, 70–200mm lens, Fuji 1600 and Fuji Provia.

Some manufacturers make infra-red film, in both colour and black-and-white varieties. Originally designed for aerial and scientific applications, other photographers soon realised the creative possibilities of these materials. They can be tricky to use – the camera needs to be loaded and unloaded in total darkness, and you will need to adjust the focus slightly to account for the different wavelength of infra-red light – but can create some really unusual pictures. It's difficult to give firm guidelines about using infra-red film, as the results vary so widely, but the black-and-white type needs to be used with a red filter while the colour type gives wildly differing colours depending on the colour of filter used. You will also find that infra-red film doesn't really work on any but bright sunny days. Learning to use these films really needs a great deal of trial-and-error experimentation.

While normal film is balanced for use in daylight, you can also buy tungsten-balanced film that is designed for use under artificial light sources. Although intended primarily for studio photographers working with tungsten lights, you will often find it useful to use this film in indoor environments lit this way, as it avoids the yellow cast that affects daylight transparency film. (You could alternatively use a correction filter but this cuts out more than a stop of light.) The colour cast is less of a problem with print film, as the printing process tends to correct it. Tungsten film used in daylight goes a very 'cold' blue colour but the creative photographer may occasionally be able to find situations in which to exploit this to produce interesting pictures.

⬆ Many museums are lit largely with tungsten lights and using film balanced for this results in pictures with correct colour rendition. I could have chosen to use flash instead, but it would have been difficult to light a large area like this evenly with a single flashgun. **Corvette museum in Effingham, Illinois, USA. Canon EOS1n, 24mm lens, Fuji 64T.**

Digital image manipulation

Just a few years ago, the retouching of photographs was the exclusive preserve of a few skilled individuals, who applied their specialised equipment and abilities to photographs intended for advertising and publication. This work was very expensive and professional photographers would go to extraordinary lengths to take images that could be used without the need for retouching, and to create special effects 'in camera'. Now anyone with a moderately powerful personal computer can effect the most remarkable transformations to their pictures.

Digital imaging has been a remarkable revolution, and to use it photographers need not shoot with digital cameras. Scanners capable of producing high-resolution digital files from photographs are available for very reasonable cost, and many camera shops offer a service whereby they will scan a number of pictures and put them on to a compact disc for just a few pounds. Once on the computer screen, the photographs can be manipulated with special software that can undertake an almost limitless range of adjustments and effects, and they can then be output using inkjet printers that produce prints of superb quality (or simply stored on hard disk or CD).

It's important, though, to appreciate what digital image manipulation can't do. It cannot transform a dull picture into a good one. It cannot

▽ 'Before' and 'after' pictures showing what can be achieved using image manipulation software. This tracking shot was taken on a motor racing circuit where there was distracting detail around almost the entire track. Having selected a sharp image, I scanned the transparency at high resolution (as the picture was to be used across two pages of a magazine) and used Adobe's Photoshop software to remove the more obvious distractions from the background before adding some blur to create more of an impression of speed. I also imported a blue sky from another transparency, to replace the blank sky on the original image.
ATS, Donington Park, Derbyshire, England. Canon EOS1n, 24mm lens, Fuji Velvia.

make an out-of-focus picture sharp, nor can it rescue a seriously under- or over-exposed image, or one with a drastic colour cast or coffee stain. Any attempt to take a photograph of a car shot in one location and superimpose it on a different background will undoubtedly look botched unless done by the most skilled operator. The underlying point here is that the wonders of digital imaging software do not mean that the photographer can forget any of his or her technical and creative skills. Great pictures still have to be produced at the taking stage, and manipulation on the computer should be limited to enhancing successful images.

Inevitably, though, there are some situations where circumstances beyond the photographer's control compromise the end result, and this is where digital imaging is most useful. It can be used to remove distracting elements from the background of a picture, a common problem with motorsport images shot at circuits crammed with advertising hoardings. It can be used to increase the contrast and colour saturation of images shot on dull days, or to remove blemishes from car bodywork, or unsightly stickers from windscreens. It can be used to improve the appearance of damaged and patched road surfaces that might otherwise spoil a great driving shot, or to take out a telegraph pole from a stunning landscape. All of these are transformations that can be easily done by a user with a few computer skills and moderate knowledge of the software.

Adobe's Photoshop program has become the industry standard for digital image manipulation, and it can perform a greater variety of transformations to photographs than any user will find a need for. It is expensive, but a limited version is often supplied with printers or scanners and this will be more than adequate for most amateur photographers. Getting the most out of a program like Photoshop inevitably involves a long period of familiarisation and practice, but the end really does justify the means.

▼ Here I used Photoshop software to remove the bollard from the background and the white lines from the road surface, before adding some motion blur. The skills necessary to effect simple transformations like these can be quickly acquired, and little detailed knowledge of computers is needed. **AC Cobra 289, Brecon Beacons, South Wales. Canon EOS1n, 300mm lens, Fuji Provia.**

Action photography and safety

Before considering the techniques for taking successful action photographs, the issue of safety needs to be addressed. Look through any car magazine and you will see dramatic pictures of cars cornering on two wheels, or oversteering wildly, or being driven a few inches from the rear of a camera car. It is important to understand that these photographs are shot by experienced

◄ This is the kind of photograph that it would be impossible to take on a public road. Working on a sprint course that had been booked specially for the shoot, I was able to use a wide-angle lens and get the driver of the car nearest to the camera to come very close to the back of the car I was in. All the cars involved were in fact driven at low speeds, and a slow shutter speed created the feeling of movement.
MGA twin-cam (in foreground) and MGA coupé, sprint course at Curborough, near Lichfield, England. Canon EOS1n, 24mm lens, Fuji Velvia.

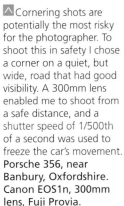
▲Cornering shots are potentially the most risky for the photographer. To shoot this in safety I chose a corner on a quiet, but wide, road that had good visibility. A 300mm lens enabled me to shoot from a safe distance, and a shutter speed of 1/500th of a second was used to freeze the car's movement. **Porsche 356, near Banbury, Oxfordshire. Canon EOS1n, 300mm lens, Fuji Provia.**

professional photographers, on closed test tracks or carefully chosen private roads, using skilled professional road testers to drive all of the cars involved. *Any attempt to recreate such pictures on public roads is a recipe for disaster, and would be foolhardy in the extreme.* No photograph is worth the slightest risk of injury to the driver, the photographer or other road users, and only the most irresponsible photographer would put him- or herself or others at risk in the cause of taking pictures.

If you are going to shoot car photographs on the road, you will need to look long and hard to find sections of road where the combination of good visibility, sufficient road width, and low volume of traffic allows pictures to be shot in absolute safety. You should always adhere to speed limits and traffic laws – this includes the wearing of seat belts – and you should display the utmost courtesy and patience towards other road users, making every effort not to distract them or hamper their progress. Even if you are fortunate enough to have access to tracks or private roads where you won't encounter other users, you should always remember that a car is potentially a

lethal weapon and that the consequences of any mishap are likely to be serious and involve death or major injury. More than one professional car photographer has suffered injury as the result of unforeseen circumstances, and every single one has tales to tell of 'near misses'. Bad weather, poor visibility or wet roads all increase the risk of accidents, and you should restrict photography to days when conditions are suitable.

Similarly, motorsport is a hazardous activity and anyone attending an event needs to be aware of the risks and to take responsibility for their own safety. At every race circuit it is abundantly clear which areas are accessible to spectators and which are out-of-bounds, and carrying a camera does not entitle you to step outside the designated areas. At events where the boundaries are not defined – such as on a rally stage – you must act responsibly and, again, carrying a camera does not confer special rights. At any form of motorsport event, you must always adhere to instructions given by marshals or other officials, and you should always remember that thoughtless or irresponsible actions might put competitors or other spectators at risk.

▲Panning shots enable the photographer to shoot from a safe distance well away from the road, but it is important to choose a quiet road to avoid distracting or impeding other motorists. This was especially the case when the passenger was a pretty model, waving at the camera. **Triumph TR5, Dartmoor, Devon, England. Canon EOS1n, 70–200mm lens, Fuji Velvia.**

Exposure for action photography

Before you attempt to shoot action photography, it is important to be thoroughly familiar with your camera equipment, and also to be sure that your exposures are going to be accurate. Whether you are shooting at a motorsport event or on the road, you are unlikely to have the opportunity to take a series of pictures at varying exposures, and there is nothing more frustrating than capturing a dramatic moment only to be disappointed with the end result because of incorrect exposure.

Accurate exposure is far more important with transparency film than with print materials. The latter have far greater exposure 'latitude', which means that you can get away with a considerable degree of under- or over-exposure and the final print will still be of acceptable quality. In contrast, transparency film has very little tolerance of incorrect exposure, and anything more than half a stop out will result in a photograph fit only for the bin.

◁ Scenes like this are problematic for a camera's meter. The large area of dark background will lead the camera to believe that there's very little light, yet the silver car is catching the last rays of winter afternoon sunshine and is very bright. By using a hand-held meter I was able to take a reading of the light falling on the scene, which disregarded the background. White and silver cars are particularly tricky to expose correctly as even slight over-exposure will cause them to appear 'bleached out' in the final image.
Audi TT, near Aberdeen, Scotland. Canon EOS1n, 70–200mm lens, Fuji Provia.

On dull days it may be necessary to 'uprate' film in order to use fast shutter speeds. The film is deliberately under-exposed and then processed for longer to compensate. Here I rated ISO 100 film at ISO 200 to enable me to shoot at 1/250th of a second; uprating by one stop does little to compromise image quality but much more than this will increase grain and reduce colour saturation. **Porsche 944, airfield at Wroughton, Wiltshire, England. Canon EOS1n, 300mm lens, Fuji Provia rated at ISO 200.**

Modern cameras have very sophisticated metering systems that can be relied upon in almost every circumstance. Shoot a hundred images with your camera in fully automatic mode and, in all probability, 99 will be perfectly exposed. Inevitably, though, as your creative skills improve you will aim to take more exciting and unusual images; a silhouette of a car cresting a brow against a dramatic sky, for example, or a shot of a rally car speeding through a woodland stage. These are exactly the kind of situations where a camera's meter might be fooled, and if you are able to recognise this likelihood you can adjust the exposure accordingly.

The ability to recognise these situations comes only with a degree of experience, but there are ways of increasing the chances of correct exposure. Most professional photographers choose not to rely on the camera's exposure meter in any but the most straightforward lighting conditions, preferring to use a hand-held meter to gauge the exposure and then transferring these settings to the camera. So why should a separate meter give more reliable exposures? The answer is that most take an 'incident' light reading; that is, they mea-sure the light falling on the subject rather than that reflected from it. This means that the read-ing is entirely unaffected by, for example, a large area of dark background that might fool a cam-era meter into over-exposing. Again, the user will need the ability to interpret readings taken with a hand-held meter but incident light readings are likely to be more accurate than reflected light ones.

Another way that professional photographers narrow the odds in their favour when using transparency film is by using a 'clip test'. A lab will, for a small additional charge, snip off and process only the first few frames of a film. This can then be carefully assessed and the remainder of the film processed accordingly. So if a clip test appears half a stop too dark, the remaining film is push-processed to compensate. This is a good means of ensuring accuracy, but the original exposure will need to be reasonably close to cor-rect, to avoid drastic adjustments at the process-ing stage (which will compromise the image quality). Clip tests are clearly of little use in light that is constantly changing, such as when clouds repeatedly obscure the sun on a windy day.

Fast-moving clouds meant that the exposure for this scene was constantly changing. However, as the car and the background were both largely even mid-tones I was able to use the camera's shutter-priority automatic mode, confident that it would give an accurate result and allowing me to concentrate on the viewfinder image. **Alfa Romeo 2900B, near Crickhowell, South Wales. Canon EOS1n, 70–200mm lens, Fuji Velvia.**

Panning 1

The easiest, and safest, technique for action photographs is panning. The photographer stands to one side of the road and 'pans' (follows) the moving car with the camera, and a shutter speed is used which will give the impression of movement while (hopefully) providing a sharp image of the car. It is a technique that can result in stunning shots, either on the road or at a race circuit, and it is well worth the practice necessary to perfect it. The key to good panning shots is a smooth pan-

ning action and this is where practice comes in.

You will need to find a viewpoint where you have a clear, uninterrupted view of the car as it passes. Ideally there will be a background behind the car which will appear blurred in the final image. An uncluttered background is best but remember that the impression of movement created in a successful shot will have the effect of hiding any small distracting elements. For a straightforward panning shot in which the whole

◁ This was an ideal location for a panning shot: a background of trees to provide an impression of movement, and a clear view of the car. There was the added advantage that the yellow car stood out well from the brown and green tones of the surroundings. I chose a time of day when the car would be in full sunlight and shot plenty of film to ensure a sharp result.
Lamborghini Countach LP400, Kemble, Gloucestershire, England. Canon EOS1n, 70–200mm lens, Fuji Velvia.

↑While panning shots often create good 'profile' images of cars, the technique can also be used to shoot front or rear three-quarter views. Here I kept my finger on the shutter button after the car had passed and was able to get this view of the distinctive lines of a Lancia Fulvia. Notice also the choice of location: an uninterrupted view and a suitable background. The fact that the car was red helped, as it was an overcast day and other colours might have resulted in a drab picture. **Lancia Fulvia 1600HF, near Bath, England. Nikon F3, 70–200mm lens, Fuji Velvia.**

car will appear sharp against the background you will need a medium telephoto lens; around 135mm or 200mm is ideal, and this is a useful situation for an 70–200mm zoom lens as you can frame the image accurately. You will then need to stand around 30 or 40 metres from where the car will pass – the exact distance will depend on the focal length of the lens and the length of the car, and you may be forced to stand further back at motorsport venues.

If you are working out on the road and have control over the situation, you will be able to brief the driver as to how you need him or her to drive past. A panning shot is much easier to achieve if the car concerned is travelling at a constant speed, as a car that is accelerating or decelerating is difficult to follow accurately. You will need, then, to ask the driver to start the approach to your camera position from some way away, so that the car's speed is steady as it passes you. (If you are shooting at a race you will need to try to find a viewpoint, such as on a straight, where the cars are passing at constant speeds. The disadvantage of this is that these

speeds are likely to be high and this can make it tricky to pan successfully.)

You will be unlikely to achieve a successful panning shot with only one 'pass' of the car, so you will need to ask the driver to make several runs and shoot several frames each time. This is where consideration is required: repeatedly turning the car in the entrance to a resident's driveway is likely to cause offence, as is rapid acceleration, especially with a noisy car. Try to find a section of road well away from houses and where the driver can turn the car easily at either end. Also avoid trampling over crops to get to your chosen viewpoint.

You will need to stand with your feet slightly apart, and face the point at which the car will pass closest to you. As the car approaches, follow it in the viewfinder, swivelling at the hips, with your finger poised over the shutter button and then, as it passes shoot a short sequence of frames using the motor drive. Continue to follow the car through the viewfinder after it has passed; this is the 'follow-through', a technique that golfers will be familiar with.

↑Pictures composed with strong diagonal lines have an inherent sense of dynamism and speed. I felt that tilting the camera while shooting this Lotus Elan made for a stronger image, and the green grass in front of and behind the car created a good colour contrast. **Lotus Elan S2, near Plymouth, Devon, England. Canon EOS1n, 70–200mm lens, Fuji Velvia.**

Panning 2

To create good panning shots, you should choose a shutter speed of around 1/60th of a second. You will notice that this is a longer speed than would be indicated by our guidelines for hand-holding telephoto lenses, where a lens's focal length determines the fraction of a second needed to hand-hold it successfully. However, the idea of a panning shot is to create an impression of movement, and if you choose to use a faster shutter speed your pictures will lack that impression. While some of your shots at 1/60th of a second will undoubtedly suffer from camera shake, the ones that work will be that much better for having used the slower speed.

This speed is only a guideline; a car travelling fast can be panned successfully at 1/125th of a second and those with a steady hand will be able to use 1/30th of a second. (And don't be afraid to experiment with longer shutter speeds; very often the best pictures come from ignoring the rulebook.) If you're using a lens longer than about 200mm however, 1/60th of a second will probably result in too many images spoiled by camera shake, so you may need to use a faster shutter speed.

Using a motor drive means that a succession of images can be shot with each pass of the car, and this considerably increases the chances of securing a sharp image in a short space of time. As with most action photography, it is tempting to rely on automatic focusing to make sure that the car is in focus, but this can have its drawbacks. For panning shots it is often preferable to compose the picture so that the car is at the top or bottom of the frame, but most cameras offer a selection of auto-focus points across the centre of the image. Also, the side view of a car may not contain sufficient fine detail for the automatic focusing to find quickly, which can result in wasted 'passes'. The best way of using manual focus for panning is to focus on a point before the car approaches and then shoot as the car passes that

⌄The arches alongside a seafront promenade provided an unusual background for this image, which was shot from close range using a 35mm lens. This is a very hit-and-miss technique and it's often necessary to shoot a lot of film to be sure of an acceptable result.
Maserati Biturbo, seafront at Brighton, East Sussex, England. Canon EOS1n, 35mm lens, Fuji Velvia.

⌄This was for a magazine feature based on the film *Get Carter* – this multi-storey car park was used as a location in the film. I chose to shoot on one of the upper floors where there were no other cars and where the car could be driven up and down without getting in anyone else's way. Bright sunlight outside the car park meant that I had to judge the exposure carefully.
Jaguar Mk II, Gateshead, Co. Durham, England. Nikon F3, 24mm lens, Fuji Provia.

point. If time allows, you can ask the driver to stop at the point where you intend to shoot beforehand, so you can focus accurately on the car while it is stationary. Remember that if you are shooting as the car passes in both directions, the focus will be slightly different for each as the car will be on different sides of the road.

As is often the case with photography, it pays to look for unusual viewpoints or locations. The basic techniques for panning shots can easily be adapted to suit different situations, and experimentation often results in original and unusual pictures. Some cars are better shot from above, while others have distinctive lines that suit front or rear views rather than side-on shots. Keep an eye open for colourful or interesting backgrounds, and make careful note of the best times of day to use different locations; if the light isn't right try to return when it is.

◁ Don't be afraid to use unusual viewpoints to create interesting pictures. Here I stood on a hillside overlooking the road, and the numerous trees and bushes meant that only short sections gave an unhindered view of the car. I followed the car through the viewfinder as it travelled along the entire length of the road, and pressed the shutter whenever I could see it clearly. Numerous passes raised the chances of a sharp result.
Maserati A6G, Monaco. Canon EOS1n, 50mm lens, Fuji Provia.

Panning 3

While a short to medium telephoto lens is ideal for shooting straightforward panning images, don't be afraid to go in closer with a shorter lens. This results in very different pictures; you won't get an end result where the whole length of the car is sharp, as different parts of the car are travelling at different speeds relative to the camera when you are in close and following the car through the viewfinder. But you can create some stunning 'effect' shots this way that have a real sense of movement and speed. Stand close to the road with a 35mm lens – or even a 28mm or 24mm lens – and concentrate hard on pressing the shutter at the ideal moment, as a car that is too far away will appear as a distant speck on the final image when you're using standard or wide-angle lenses. Shoot plenty of film and select your final image from the results with care. Pictures where the entire car is blurred are rarely successful; at least part of the car should be sharp.

◁ To illustrate a feature comparing an Alfa Romeo SZ and RZ I opted for a two-car panning shot that would show the differing profiles of both cars. Fortunately this section of road, in the New Forest, is ideally suited as it is dead straight for almost a mile and has little traffic on it outside of holiday periods. This was the only picture from three films where both cars were sharp. **Alfa Romeo SZ (front) and RZ, New Forest, Hampshire, England. Canon EOS1n, 70–200mm lens, Fuji Provia.**

While panning is a very simple technique for shooting single cars, using two or more cars is more difficult. Finding a suitable road is much harder, as to get cars side-by-side you need a wide road that is long and straight, with exceptional visibility and little or no other traffic. (Shooting with cars one in front of the other rarely gives dramatic pictures.) If you are attempting this on public roads, you will need to be acutely aware of the possible risks associated with driving cars abreast across the road. Drivers need to understand exactly what you are trying to achieve and have to be able to position the cars accurately while moving, and to hold those positions while passing the camera position.

To get a clear enough view of the cars, one of them – usually that furthest from the camera – will need to be slightly ahead of the other, and this a very difficult position for the drivers to adopt and maintain. The speeds of both cars will need to be closely synchronised, and their positions taken on the approach to the photographer (a long approach makes this easier). If the cars are moving relative to each other it will be impossible to shoot an image where both cars are sharp, so the driver of the car in front should attain the required speed and maintain it while the other driver manoeuvres into place and holds that position exactly while passing the photographer. To be sure of getting a successful picture you will need plenty of passes and to shoot lots of film, and inevitably the presence of other traffic will disrupt the whole procedure.

Panning shots using more than two cars are more complicated still to set up, and are unlikely to be done successfully unless you have access to a test track or similar location where there is plenty of space and no possibility of encountering other cars.

Panning 4

Once you've mastered the basic techniques for panning shots, you will undoubtedly want to expand your creative horizons and think about ways of making more interesting and unusual images. Because panning is a technique that can be done in relative safety, it lends itself well to different methods.

One of the best ways of improving any driving shot is to combine a long exposure with flash.

This is a particularly useful technique for dull or wet days, when the available light alone would tend to give rather lifeless images. You can select a long shutter speed that would, on its own, give an unacceptably blurred image but then add flash to create a sharp image of the car. It's important to learn how to balance the exposure for the flash with that for the available light, and in most circumstances the flash will act as a fill-in

◁ On a sprint course shrouded in thick fog, drastic measures were needed to make interesting pictures. I used a shutter speed of 1/8th of a second and added flash to brighten the whole image. A wide-angle lens was necessary, as with a telephoto the car was barely visible through the fog! I tilted the camera to give the image strong diagonal lines and an 85B filter helped prevent the predominantly cold blue tones that often result when shooting on foggy days.
Alfasud 1.5 Sprint Trofeo, sprint course at Curborough, near Lichfield, Staffordshire, England. Canon EOS1n, 24mm lens, 85B warm-up filter, Metz 60CT-4 flash, Fuji Velvia.

I used flash as fill-in on this shot of a trials car negotiating an off-road course. The effect of the flash is subtle but can be noticed on the wheel nearest the camera, and on the number plate. (Modern reflective number plates often appear much too bright when lit with flash.) A shutter speed of 1/30th of a second gave the necessary impression of movement.
Liege trials car, in a field in Oxfordshire, England. Canon EOS1n, 24mm lens, Metz 60CT-4, Fuji Velvia.

rather than as the main light source. To achieve this, you will need to set the flash to give a correct exposure for an aperture one or two stops wider than that you are using. (So if you are shooting at f/8, set the flash to f/5.6 or f/4.) This way, the flash exposure will be enough to pick up detail in the car and improve the colour saturation but it won't take over and make a driving shot look like a static – this can easily happen if, for example, the flash exposure is bright enough to 'freeze' the movement of the car's wheels. To master this technique, shoot a series of pictures with the flash at different settings, making a note of the exposures and then carefully checking the results.

A natural extension of this technique is to try shooting at night. In contrast, here the flash will often be the main light source and the long exposure will record any point sources of light, such as distant streetlights, as trails. Set the flash to expose correctly for the lens aperture and

then choose the shutter speed according to the effect you wish to achieve (and remember that, when there is virtually no available light, you can choose almost any shutter speed and it will make little difference to the exposure for the car). Again, experimentation is the key to success: try shooting at as many different settings as time allows.

One word of warning about using flash to shoot motorsport: a burst of powerful flash can be extremely distracting for a driver who isn't expecting it. While flash used for a side view of passing car is unlikely to cause a problem, a flash directly into a driver's eyes can be very dangerous. While rally drivers may well be used to driving through wooded stages with flashes popping from all directions, a flash fired directly in front of the car on a night stage would probably ruin a driver's night vision and could lead to a serious accident. Always act responsibly in such circumstances.

This was shot on a deserted roundabout late at night. I asked the driver to keep driving round and then shot a series of pictures using various shutter speeds; the exposure here was two seconds and this has recorded the distant lights as trails, which gives a sense of speed. I set the flash to one stop less than the lens aperture as I wanted to avoid over-exposing the road in the foreground.
Lamborghini Diablo SV, London Docklands, England. Canon EOS1n, 35mm lens, Metz 60CT-4 flash, Fuji Provia.

Tracking 1

Look through any car magazine and you will see pictures of cars that have been taken, while on the move, from another vehicle. This is known as 'tracking', and it is a remarkably effective means of shooting cars that can provide some of the most dramatic pictures. However, it also carries inherent risks that you should be aware of before attempting the technique for yourself. Driving cars close together, in formation, for photography requires skilled and careful driving on the part of both drivers, and has to be done with the utmost regard to the safety of those involved as well as other road users.

To shoot tracking shots safely on public roads, you will have to look long and hard to find a road that is suitable. It needs to be dead straight for a long distance, with good visibility along the entire length of the straight, and also needs to be wide enough to position the cars in an appropriate formation to allow for photography. It needs to be free of other traffic, and a smooth road surface is important to help reduce the risk of cam-

◁ This rare and very valuable car was shot at a private test track, which meant that I was able to experiment with different techniques and unusual angles. I used a waist-level viewfinder and held the camera down close to the road to get this dramatic view. Focusing was tricky through the viewfinder (I was using a non-auto-focus camera) so I pre-set the focus and then used hand signals to direct the driver into the correct position. **Ferrari 250 GTO, test track near Uttoxeter, Staffordshire, England. Nikon F3 with waist-level viewfinder, 24mm lens, Fuji Provia.**

It's tempting to think that dual carriageway roads would be ideal for tracking shots, as they allow cars to travel abreast without the risk of meeting oncoming traffic. The reality is that most dual carriageway roads are busy during daylight hours and you will annoy impatient motorists by occupying both lanes to take photographs. This Mercedes SSK was difficult to manoeuvre and fortunately we were able to find a quiet stretch of dual carriageway, but we frequently had to let other drivers pass.
Mercedes SSK, near Stuttgart, Germany. Canon EOS1n, 35mm lens, Fuji Velvia.

era shake. On today's increasingly congested roads, finding suitable locations for tracking shots is very difficult. Look again at those magazines and you will spot that many of the photographs have noticeably similar backgrounds; that's because a great many of the magazines use the same few test tracks to shoot their tracking shots in safety. However, there are roads that can be used safely and if you choose your time carefully there's no reason why you shouldn't be able to try this technique for yourself.

Clearly you will need a 'camera car' in addition to the car you're shooting, and as well as allowing you to photograph in safety this should ideally have a smooth ride, as holding a camera steady while moving along is difficult. You will need to use reasonably slow shutter speeds to create an impression of movement and you will find that your pictures have a good sense of movement even at 20 or 30 miles per hour, and camera shake is more of a problem at higher speeds. Whether you choose to shoot from out

of a car window or from a hatchback that is propped open, you will need to wear a seat belt and to be in a secure position. Before starting, make sure both drivers know the positions they will have to adopt – if you can place the cars in the correct formation before moving off then everyone will be sure of what they're doing and you can frame your shot accurately.

Once you set off, get the subject car to move quickly into position. If one car or the other moves to the 'wrong' side of the road you will have a good three-quarter view of the subject (hence the need for a wide, straight road and good visibility). Shoot as many frames as you can while the cars are able to maintain the appropriate positions, and make sure that everyone moves back to the correct side well before you run out of road. With a subject car close to the rear bumper, the driver of the camera car will have to avoid braking sharply and you should always make sure there is a big margin for error at every stage of the procedure.

Don't be afraid to include plenty of the road and the scenery in your composition, as this can help with the sense of speed. This deserted Welsh mountain road made an interesting backdrop and I used a wide-angle lens to give the impression of driving on open roads through a rugged landscape.
Lancia Delta Integrale, near Dolgellau, North Wales. Nikon F3, 24mm lens, Fuji Provia.

Tracking 2

When you are looking for a suitable road for tracking, it's important to remember that as well as satisfying the safety criteria it should also make for great pictures. Avoid roads that have cluttered backgrounds, or abundant telegraph poles and road signs. Look also for roads that don't have too many painted lines, or tarmac that has been extensively patched. Ideally you will need a background that will appear blurred on the finished picture, so look for roads that have high hedges or lines of trees alongside them. (A distant sky or landscape won't blur enough to give an impression of movement.)

Choose a standard lens if possible: a tele-

◁ This picture was taken for the front cover of a magazine; the car was a competition prize and pretty girls help sell more magazines! I used a flashgun connected to the camera while another inside the car was connected to a slave unit (to trigger it simultaneously), and was used to light the girl. We drove back and forth around this corner, shooting plenty of film, and the lateral movement of cornering has helped to create a feeling of speed. I was using a wide-angle lens and with the Mini close to the back of the camera car both drivers had to concentrate hard. **Mini Cooper, near March, Cambridgeshire, England. Canon EOS1n, 24mm lens, Metz 60CT-4 and 45CT-5 flashes, Fuji Velvia.**

This Rolls-Royce was photographed for a magazine, with a couple dressed for a night at the opera, and it was important to continue the theme throughout the feature. I used a slaved flash inside the car to light the couple and an exposure of one second blurred the street lights. This helped to disguise the modern cars parked alongside the road, which would have spoiled the 'period' feel of the shoot. Rolls-Royce Phantom III, central London, England. Nikon F3, 24mm lens, Metz 60CT-4 and 45CT-5 flashes, Fuji Provia.

photo lens will result in pictures without a good sense of movement and is prone to camera shake, while with a wide-angle lens you may well end up with a car that is too small in the frame unless the driver of the subject car is confident enough to drive very close to the camera car. A 35mm lens is ideal. Set a shutter speed of around 1/60th of a second; this will give a reasonable 'hit rate' of sharp results but will still give an impression of speed. On smooth roads and with a steady hand you may be able to use 1/30th of a second and this makes for more dramatic pictures. A motor drive will enable you to shoot plenty of pictures once the cars are in formation, and automatic focusing will leave you with one less thing to worry about. A graduated grey filter is often useful when shooting tracking, to retain detail in a bright sky that might otherwise be a distraction.

You are looking, on the final picture, for a car that is pin-sharp against a blurred background. This means that you will need to shoot plenty of film to ensure success, although a smooth road and/or a car with a good ride will help. On a less than perfect road, a 'hit-rate' of only two or

three sharp frames on a 36-exposure film is not unusual! (And you can bet that one of those will have a distracting road sign in the background…) If you are going to go back and forth along the same road taking pictures, try to find convenient turning places where you can turn both cars safely and quickly (always remembering the need for courtesy to residents).

Once you have mastered the technique, you can aim to shoot more interesting images. Consider adding flash (balancing the flash exposure and the available light in the manner already described), or using wide-angle lenses to include more of the surroundings in your pictures. The more of the road you include in your composition, the more pronounced the 'groundrush' effect will be and it is this which gives the impression of movement. Try shooting from different viewpoints or unusual angles, always remembering the need to act responsibly. Experiment with different shutter speeds, although bear in mind that, as with panning, tracking shots where the car is completely blurred don't really work. Always keep your eyes open for stretches of road that offer opportunities for unusual pictures.

A road tunnel provided an unusual backdrop for this Lancia. I used a magenta filter on the camera to correct the fluorescent lighting in the tunnel and this meant that I had to place a green filter over the flash (otherwise the flash would have given a magenta cast to the foreground). An exposure of ½ a second provided the blur but the flash made sure that the side of the car remained sharp. Lancia Fulvia HF coupé, Limehouse link tunnel, east London, England. Canon EOS1n, 24mm lens, CC30M filter, Metz 60CT-4 flash with green filter, Fuji Provia.

Tracking 3

Tracking shots need not be exclusively of the front of a car. Many cars have distinctive rear views and tracking is a good technique for taking action shots of this angle, although some slight changes of technique are necessary. You will need to shoot from the passenger seat of the camera car and from this viewpoint it is very difficult to get a good view of a car that is on the opposite side of the road. This means that the subject car will need to stay on the

◀ A quiet, straight road bordered by a high hedge provided the perfect setting for shooting the rear view of this beautiful 1930s Alfa Romeo, and the red paint was a good contrast with the vivid green hedge. I used a shutter speed of 1/30th of a second with a wide-angle lens to give the sense of speed. The summer afternoon sunlight meant that I could only shoot going in this direction, as in the other I was facing into the light and the bright colours were lost. This meant that both cars had to be repeatedly turned round until enough film had been shot to be sure of a successful result.
Alfa Romeo 6C 1750, near South Cerney, Gloucestershire, England. Canon EOS1n, 24mm lens, Fuji Velvia.

 To get a dramatic shot of the rear of this Ferrari Dino I used a waist-level viewfinder and held the camera down as low as I could from the passenger window of the camera car. A deserted Welsh mountain road enabled me to shoot plenty of film, as this technique was rather hit-and-miss, especially when it came to ensuring the car was in focus. I used a graduated grey filter to retain tone in the sky and an 81A warm-up helped to enhance the red of the car. **Ferrari Dino 246 GT, Brecon Beacons, South Wales. Nikon F3, 24mm lens, graduated grey and 81A warm-up filters, Fuji Provia.**

'correct' (legal) side of the road and the camera car driver will need to move into an 'overtaking' position for you to get a rear three-quarter view of the subject.

Once again, both drivers need to be accurately briefed and a suitable speed agreed on before starting. From a driver's seat, positioning a car close to the offside rear corner of another is difficult; you will need to look closely through the viewfinder and shout instructions to the camera car driver. As ever, both drivers need to be concentrating as much on the road ahead as on photography and be ready to respond quickly should an oncoming vehicle suddenly appear. In order to lean far enough out of the car window to shoot you may need to kneel on the seat rather sit on it. You should, however, wear a seat belt at all times, and it is advisable to lock the car door you are shooting from in case it flies open as you lean on it. Keep spare film and other lenses close to hand – this will save you rummaging around for something when you need it quickly.

As with front tracking shots, a 35mm lens works well although you may find that a wide-angle gives more exciting images, if your camera car driver has the confidence to go close enough. Again, a shutter speed of 1/60th of a second will give a reasonable success rate but try to use 1/30sec when circumstances allow. This is another situation where a burst of flash can add life to your pictures, and this will allow you to experiment with the combination of flash and long shutter speeds.

You will also find that looking through the camera's viewfinder is very much more difficult when shooting looking forwards; the oncoming rush of air will make your eyes water at anything above a fast walking pace. Cold days exacerbate the problem. Focusing is tricky – you can get round this by either pre-setting the focus or relying on auto-focus. Watch carefully that you don't have a corner of the camera car's bonnet, or door mirror, in your viewfinder as you shoot. Look out, also for shadows of the camera car. These can easily spoil an otherwise good picture and need to be borne in mind when you are location hunting. Work out at what time of day the sun will light the car effectively without distracting shadows, and plan your visit accordingly.

Working at a test track meant that I could get in close with a wide-angle lens and shoot looking right over the driver's shoulder and into the cockpit. I used flash to retain sharpness in the side of the car but I had to be careful that this only acted as fill-in – too much light from the flash would have 'frozen' the spokes of the rear wheel and made it look as though the car was stationary. **MG 'Parson Special', test track at Chobham, Surrey. Nikon F3, 24mm lens, Metz 60CT-4 flash, Fuji Velvia.**

Tracking 4

Tracking can also be used to shoot more than one car at a time. Here the need for deserted roads and good visibility are especially acute; manoeuvring two or more cars into the necessary positions for photography is very tricky and requires skilled driving, and just as important is the ability to quickly break formation and return to safety. Most professional photographers, when asked to provide multi-car tracking shots, will opt to work at a test track or race circuit as there are very few stretches of road where these can be shot as safely and efficiently as on a private facility.

Attempting to shoot more than two cars at a time on a public road is not recommended, and there are other reasons for this than the obvious safety concerns. It is very difficult to get anything resembling a dramatic tracking shot involving more than two cars. Multi-car set-ups tend to

◁ Wherever possible you should aim to find roads like this for tracking shots. As well as being wide and dead straight, both sides of the road have clean, uncluttered surroundings; there are no white lines and the tarmac surface is smooth and even-toned. When shooting an image like this, always ask the faster car to adopt the position on the wrong side of the road, as it will be able to accelerate quickly into place as soon as the road is clear.
BMW 328 (in foreground) and AC Ace Bristol, near Swindon, Wiltshire, England. Canon EOS1n, 35mm lens, graduated grey filter, Fuji Velvia.

This was shot for a feature comparing a road-spec Lancia Stratos to a rally car. I wanted the bright green car in the foreground, and working on a summer day I waited until early evening when the sun was lower in the sky, as this made the light more interesting. Again a road without white lines made for a cleaner shot. **Lancia Stratos road car (in foreground) and 1977 East African Safari rally car, near Rosenburg, Austria. Canon EOS1n, 24mm lens, Fuji Velvia.**

look like static shots, and it is difficult to inject a sense of movement into such pictures. Also there will be large gaps between the cars however you arrange them and these will be more apparent on the final image. The only way to get a strong image of three or four cars is to arrange them abreast, close together across the width of the road (shooting from low down with a wide-angle lens), and this is clearly impossible on virtually every public road.

With care, though, there is no reason why you shouldn't attempt two-car tracking shots on a suitable road. Inevitably these pictures involve one car being on the 'wrong' side of the road, and all the drivers will need to be sure of exactly which positions they are to adopt for the photograph, and the sequence by which they are to drop back to safe positions afterwards. It's virtually impossible to get a good two-car rear tracking shot without including the bonnet of the camera car so it's best to stick to front views.

You'll need to shoot at low speeds, as positioning the cars is time-consuming and moving quickly you'll run out of road before shooting any pictures.

There are several different ways of composing two-car tracking shots. You can choose to have both cars side-by-side with their noses level, and by asking your driver to position the camera car in the middle of the road this gives a dramatic image. Alternatively you can opt to have one car ahead of the other, and by keeping the camera car on the correct side of the road this gives a front-on view of one car with a three-quarter view of the other. Bear in mind that if you use a wide-angle lens for this type of shot that the car furthest from the camera will appear quite small in the frame. Work out exactly how you want to compose your shot before you start, and if possible arrange the cars in the viewfinder while stationary before you set off down the road.

These two Jaguars were shot for a magazine's front cover and this required the use of the upright format. I tilted the camera to make a more dramatic picture, and the area of tarmac in the foreground allowed for type to be inserted in this space. The high viewpoint was achieved by shooting from the hatchback of a 'people carrier' with the hatch securely propped open. A sprint course was booked exclusively for the shoot and this meant that we were able to work in safety. **Jaguar XK120 (in foreground) and XK150, sprint course at Curborough, near Lichfield, Staffordshire, England. Canon EOS1n, 24mm lens, Fuji Velvia.**

Cornering 1

There are two reasons why cars – both on the road and racing – are photographed as they drive through a corner. The first is that to 'freeze' a car moving at even moderate pace requires a very fast shutter speed, and it is necessary to shoot at a point where the car's speed is at its lowest. The second is that cornering makes for the most interesting pictures, as the forces acting on the car as it turns cause it to lean over, creating an impression of movement that would be absent if the car were photographed while travelling in a straight line. However, taking cornering pictures carries the greatest potential danger for the photographer.

A car travelling in a straight line is unlikely to deviate from its course except in extreme circumstances, but a car taking a corner quickly may easily lose grip, with possibly disastrous consequences for a photographer in a vulnerable position. When choosing a location, and a

◁ Although this car is leaning hard, it was in fact travelling very slowly. The corner was exceptionally tight and the car could only get round at low speed yet still looked dramatic. This stretch of road had the added advantages that it was very quiet, with exceptional visibility, and had a good background that was not only uncluttered but provided a contrast to the car. Even in relatively safe circumstances like this, it is important to use a long lens, which allows shooting from a distance. Lotu Elan +2, near Malvern, Worcestershire, England. Nikon F3, 300mm lens, Fuji Provia.

⌃Cornering shots always look best from a very low viewpoint. Here I was lying flat on the ground, and this has resulted in a picture where the car is clearly leaning as it passes through the corner. (It is always worth packing a mat or similar to lie on, especially when the ground is wet!) A quiet road allowed shooting in safety and provided a good clean background. **Aston Martin Lagonda Series 2, near Newport Pagnell, Buckinghamshire, England. Canon EOS1n 300mm lens, Fuji Provia.**

viewpoint, for cornering, you must always be mindful of the need for safety. Inevitably the best viewpoint for a cornering shot will always be one that is directly in the path of a car that has lost control. At race venues it is likely that there will be tyre walls, fencing and other measures in place to protect spectators but racing cars travel at high speeds and there is always the potential for an accident.

Out on the road there will be no such safety measures and it is essential that you not only choose your position with care, but also use a long telephoto lens that enables you to shoot from a reasonable distance. Wet or icy roads significantly increase the risks and you should shoot only when conditions are appropriate.

When shooting on the roads, you will need to have absolute faith in the driver of the car. Any attempt at 'showing off' for the camera is likely to have disastrous consequences, not just for the photographer (and the car and driver) but also

for other road users. You will need to find a corner on a quiet road and it is essential that this has excellent visibility, enabling the driver to see clearly as he or she approaches the corner if there is any oncoming traffic. Before starting you should ensure that the car is in good working order and that tyre pressures are correct, as poorly inflated tyres can compromise the car's ability to corner safely.

It's best to find a really tight corner, as this allows good pictures to be taken in safety. A car taking a sharp corner will lean dramatically, even at low speeds. In contrast, a modern car taking a gentle, sweeping bend at speed may hardly lean at all, and there is always the possibility that pictures taken in these circumstances will look as though the car was stationary. Always make sure that you choose a corner that has a clean, uncluttered background. Road signs, lampposts, fences or railings can all appear as distractions on the finished photograph.

⌃Here I chose to use the camera in an upright position, to include some of the mountain scenery. Again the car was only travelling slowly, but the sense of speed is provided by the fact that the corner was sharp, and also because the driver has struck a convincing pose that makes it look as though he is working hard to steer the car. Notice also that the driver is wearing an appropriate outfit; modern clothing would have looked completely out of place in a car like this. **1922 Targa Florio Mercedes, Monaco. Nikon F3, 300mm lens, Fuji Provia.**

Cornering 2

Cornering shots present more technical challenges than any other type of action image. To shoot cornering effectively you will certainly need a long telephoto lens, and mastery of shutter speeds and focusing. Anything less than a 200mm lens, if used from a safe distance, will result in an image that has the car too small in the frame. Most professional photographers will use a lens of at least 300mm for this type of shot, and even this won't be long enough at most motor racing venues. A motor drive is also essential; you will need to shoot a sequence of images as the car passes through the corner to be sure of getting the best image and this is only possible with a motor drive capable of several frames a second.

You will also need to use a fast shutter speed to capture the image; 1/250th of a second is the longest speed that will be capable of freezing the car's motion, and wherever possible you should try to use 1/500th or even 1/1000th of a second. This means that you will often have to turn to fast films, particularly in overcast conditions. The alternative is to uprate and 'push-process' slower film, or to use a lens with a wide

maximum aperture, and this is why so many professional car photographers are prepared to invest in 300mm or 400mm lenses with maximum apertures of f/2.8.

Focusing has to be absolutely spot-on. With the extremely narrow depth-of-field inherent with a long lens, a fast-moving car will travel through the point of focus in a tiny fraction of a second. There are two ways of attempting to capture a sharp image: you can rely on automatic focusing, or you can pre-focus and hope to shoot at the exact moment that the car is sharp. Modern auto-focus systems have a 'servo' mode that will keep up with a fast-moving car, and combined with a motor drive, this can result in a sequence of pin-sharp images. However, in dull weather or when shooting some subjects, auto-focus may not work effectively and this is where it is useful to be familiar with the technique of pre-focusing. Here you use manual focusing, and set the focus before the car appears. It is usually best to focus on a spot just in front of the apex of the corner, as this is where the car will look at its most dramatic. As soon as the car appears, you press the shutter button (using the motor drive

◁ Fast shutter speeds are essential for shots like this. This image was shot at 1/1000th of a second; look carefully beneath the car and you can see the small stones 'frozen' as they are thrown up by the tyres. The corner was chosen because it had a clean background that would help the car to stand out, and I was lying on the ground as this is nearly always the best view of a cornering car. I was using a non-auto-focus camera and used the pre-focus technique. This meant that the driver had to make several passes but on a deserted road this wasn't a problem. **Ferrari 365GTC, New Forest, Hampshire, England. Nikon F3, 300mm lens, Fuji Provia.**

▶This sequence of pictures shows the pre-focusing technique. I chose to focus at a point where the car would fill the frame just after passing the apex of the corner, and then hit the shutter button as soon as the car appeared in the viewfinder. With a motor drive shooting at six frames per second the series includes pictures taken before and after the car was in focus. Look carefully and you will see that in the fourth frame of the sequence (frame 19) the front of the car is pin-sharp while it is slightly out-of-focus on the others. **BMW 2002 Turbo, sprint course at Curborough, near Lichfield, Staffordshire, England. Canon EOS1n, 300mm lens, Fuji Provia.**

▶I deliberately chose a dusty section of road for this shot, as the dust kicked up by the wheels adds to the feeling of speed. On a bright day, and with a car with plenty of detail across its front, automatic focusing was easily able to keep track of the car and this resulted in a sharp series of pictures from which I was able to select the best one. **Voisin C28 Aérosport, near Stansted Airport, Essex, England. Canon EOS1n, 300mm lens, Fuji Velvia.**

on its fastest setting) and shoot several frames as the car travels through the corner. With luck, one of those frames will have captured the car exactly at the point of focus. You will need several 'passes' to be sure of a successful image, and of course, when shooting motor racing this won't always be possible.

Many skilled professional motorsport photographers have perfected their pre-focusing technique to the extent that they can shoot just one frame as the car corners, but this is extremely difficult to get right, as an SLR camera takes a sizeable fraction of a second to release the shutter after the button is pressed. If you shoot when you can see the car is sharp you will miss the shot, as by the time the mirror flips up and the shutter opens the car will have long passed the point of focus. The skill here is in accurate anticipation, and until you have acquired this skill it is better to rely on shooting several frames.

Cornering 3

Cornering shots don't really allow the same opportunities for experimentation that other types of action pictures do. It's not really possible, for example, to add flash as shooting with a long lens the flash won't reach the car, and in any case it is virtually impossible to shoot one frame at the exact spot that the car is in focus. (Shooting a quick sequence of frames won't give the flash time to recharge.) You can try the effects of different shutter speeds but, as with panning and tracking shots, images where the entire car is blurred are rarely successful.

◄ This picture was actually the result of a happy accident. Having just finished shooting panning shots of the car, we moved on to shoot cornering. The car appeared before I was quite ready and I quickly put the camera to my eye and, after shooting a sequence as it came around the corner, I realised that the shutter speed was still set to 1/30th of a second. I changed to a faster speed for the next pass but looking through the results, this image stood out. **Jensen Interceptor, North Yorkshire Moors, Yorkshire, England. Canon EOS1n, 300mm lens, Fuji Velvia.**

The most important difference is that automatic focusing is much less likely to secure a sharp image. Auto-focus that can readily keep up with an approaching car seems, for some reason, to struggle with a car moving away from the camera. Even when it does succeed in following the car it seems to take much longer between frames to find the car's new position and this inevitably leads to missed pictures. To be sure of getting a sharp end result you will need to pre-focus and, where possible, ask the driver to make several runs. It helps, if circumstances allow, to ask the driver to stop the car at the most appropriate position on the road before you start. You can then frame your shot and pre-focus accurately on the car.

△ A straightforward rear cornering shot shows the distinctive back of this Aston Martin. I pre-focused, choosing to focus on a spot at the apex of the corner so that some of the car's side would be visible. This view is usually preferable to a straight rear view.
Aston Martin DB5, test track at Chobham, Surrey, England. Canon EOS1n, 300mm lens, Fuji Provia.

▽ For this rear cornering shot I asked the girl to look back towards the camera to make the picture more interesting. Although the car was actually travelling quite quickly it didn't lean much through the corner and as a consequence there's not much sense of speed to the picture.
Ferrari 250GT Cabriolet Series II, near Cassis, South of France. Canon EOS1n, 300mm lens, Fuji Provia.

The techniques described so far have been directed at getting good cornering shots of cars travelling towards the photographer. There will be occasions when there is a need to shoot a car moving in the opposite direction, and although most of the methods remain the same there are a few essential differences. The first thing to note is that this technique carries a far lower degree of risk for the photographer, as if the car loses grip it will leave the road well away from the photographer. This is not an excuse for more extreme driving, as the consequences of an accident are still potentially serious, but it does mean that the photographer has greater freedom when it comes to choosing a viewpoint. It is, however, still preferable to use a long lens, as you will need to fill the frame with the car and the narrow depth-of-field helps to throw the background out-of-focus. (This has the added advantage that any potentially distracting elements in the background will be less noticeable.) You will still need to use a fast shutter speed to be sure of an image where the car is sharp, and again the best pictures will usually be shot from a low viewpoint; try lying or crouching down.

Off-road action

Shooting cars off-road can be a recipe for some great pictures. The basic techniques are the same as for other forms of action photography but some modification may be necessary for the different circumstances found when shooting in knee-deep mud and water. The first point to make is that you should only drive off-road where this is permitted. Users of four-wheel drive vehicles have acquired a bad reputation for churning up areas of the countryside and trespassing, and you should not overstep the mark just in order to take photographs. The more off-roaders behave irresponsibly, the more rules and regulations – and physical barriers – will be put in

◁ On a miserable wet December day, I used flash to add sparkle to this shot of a Land Rover hitting a puddle. I tilted the camera to create a strong diagonal in the picture, and asked the driver – an experienced off-roader – to make several passes, as I could only shoot one frame each time to allow for the flash to recharge. The flash has 'frozen' the puddle effectively but there is plenty of blur in the background.
Land Rover Series I, by-way on Salisbury Plain, Wiltshire, England. Canon EOS1n, 35mm lens, Metz 60CT-4 flash, Fuji Provia.

△This was taken at a special off-road course where there were plenty of opportunities for exciting pictures. I used a long lens and shot a sequence of frames with the motor drive as the Land Rover made its way through the puddle. Winter afternoon sunlight provided the warm tones.
Land Rover Series I, off-road course in Nottinghamshire, England. Canon EOS1n, 70–200mm lens, Fuji Velvia.

place to stop them, and thoughtless actions may spoil things for future visitors. There are plenty of by-ways, 'green lanes' and special off-road courses where you can enjoy the pleasures of off-road driving without causing offence.

When it comes to photography, the most important difference, compared with shooting on the road, is that speeds will be much lower. So for effective panning shots, you will probably need to use slower shutter speeds and a more imaginative approach to end up with strong pictures. You are also unlikely to be able to take successful tracking shots, as bouncing about in the back of a four-wheel-drive vehicle is not compatible with avoiding excessive camera shake! Concentrate on taking imaginative pictures from outside the vehicle, and look for key ingredients such as steep banks, deep puddles and liquid mud to capture the essence of off-roading. (But don't ask a driver to do anything their vehicle isn't capable of doing in safety just because it might make a good picture.)

The winter months are likely to be more rewarding for this kind of photography, and a sunny day after prolonged rain will probably result in ideal conditions, allowing for bright pic-

tures of off-road vehicles up to their axles in mud. Although you are unlikely to take true cornering shots off-road, the same techniques – long lens, fast shutter speed and auto-focus – work well to create sharp pictures of four-wheel-drive vehicles as they plough through mud and puddles. Look for opportunities to take striking head-on shots in such situations, and where possible ask the driver to make several passes.

While for most car photography the subject should usually be as clean as possible, this is certainly not the case off-road and a vehicle that has already had a good thrash through the mud will make for far more authentic-looking pictures than one which has been carefully driven from the nearest tarmac.

Snow and ice can also provide opportunities for great driving pictures. After a fresh snowfall find somewhere with plenty of space (and no other cars to hit) and you can take images of cars sliding around which will look dramatic but can all be done at low speed and in safety, providing you choose a long lens and stay well out of the car's way. Remember that large areas of snow in the frame will fool a camera's meter into underexposing so make allowances for this.

△For a feature about driving a Caterham to the Alps in winter, we found a deserted car park covered in fresh snow, and chose a viewpoint that gave a good background. The driver then drove round in circles at low speed, allowing the car to slide, as I shot from a safe distance with a long lens.
Caterham 7, near Val d'Isère, French Alps. Canon EOS1n, 70–200mm lens, Fuji Provia.

Other action techniques 1

There are other ways of shooting action pictures that don't really fit into any of the previous categories. Professional photographers often shoot from inside the car, or attach cameras to the outside of the car, as a means of taking unusual and original images. This way you can use long exposures to create a sense of movement, and there are endless possibilities for the creative photographer to exploit.

It's often useful to combine flash with a long exposure, in order to retain sharpness in at least some of the image, and this is a technique that works particularly well with car interiors. Shoot from the back seat of the car, and try to get as far back as possible to include the whole width of the dashboard. If you base your exposure on the available light outside the car, the interior would normally be under-exposed. By adding a burst of

◁ For this photograph I used a tripod, with its legs fully extended but closed together. This was wedged behind the car's passenger seat and held securely by the seat belt and several bungee cords. I mounted a camera with a 20mm lens and flashgun on the tripod, and focused carefully. Working on a deserted section of road surrounded by trees, on an overcast afternoon, the correct exposure on ISO 50 film was one second at f/8 but I set the flash to f/5.6, so that it would act as fill-in. With the car stationary, I leaned across and set the camera's self-timer, then drove off slowly. By the time the shutter opened, I was doing no more than 10mph but the one second exposure has blurred the surroundings to give an impression of speed.
Mazda MX-5, near Crowthorne, Berkshire, England. Canon EOS-5, 20mm lens, Metz 45CT-5 flash, Fuji Velvia.

which to work. Although these lenses give plenty of depth-of-field you should ensure that you focus carefully, as it can be difficult to see through the viewfinder inside a dark car and there is nothing more frustrating than spending time working to create an unusual picture only for the results to be spoiled by poor focus.

The best way of ensuring success is to shoot plenty of film, using different shutter speeds and flash settings. Make sure that the flash is not reflected in the windscreen or rear-view mirror, and watch also for distracting objects left in glove compartments or door pockets, as you may not notice them at the time of shooting but they will undoubtedly be obvious on the finished picture. Try bouncing the flash off the car's interior roof lining, as a means of softening the light.

⏷ Working in the half-hour after sunset, there was a good colour in the sky but light levels were low enough that I could use an exposure of one second. This has helped to blur distracting detail, such as parked cars, alongside the road. Here the flash has acted as the primary light source for the car's interior, which means that it is pin-sharp despite the one-second exposure. **Maserati Biturbo, Brighton seafront, East Sussex, England. Canon EOS1n, 20mm lens, Metz 60CT-4 flash, Fuji Provia.**

⏶ Here I sat on the car's rather cramped back seat, with a camera and a 20mm lens. As we drove along I shot a sequence of pictures using a shutter speed of 1/15th of a second. The bumpy road surface meant that I was bouncing around in the back of the car and this has helped give the picture its sense of movement while fill-in flash has kept the dashboard sharp. **Mercedes-Benz 190SL, Monaco. Canon EOS1n, 20mm lens, Metz 60CT-4 flash, Fuji Provia.**

flash you can make sure that it is correctly exposed, and with care you can balance the flash and the available light to create outstanding pictures. The flash needs to act as fill-in, rather than as the main light source, so you may need to set it to an aperture one or two stops wider than that set on the lens. (So if you are shooting at f/8 set the flash to f/4 or f/5.6.) In order to use a long shutter speed to create a sense of movement, you may need to find a piece of road where there is little available light. Roads surrounded by thick woods work particularly well; even on sunny days you may be able to use a shutter speed of ¼ or ½ a second which will give plenty of blur. (The flash will eliminate the possibility of camera shake spoiling the picture.) You could also try shooting at night, or in the early evening, when there is little available light and when streetlights or other cars' lights will produce attractive trails of light on the finished picture.

For these kinds of picture you will need a wide-angle lens; it is in these circumstances when lenses as wide as 20mm have their uses, as car interiors are inevitably cramped spaces in

Other action techniques 2

While there are numerous established means of shooting action pictures, these should by no means be viewed as the limit of what is possible.

The creative photographer will always be looking for new ways of tackling any subject, and experimentation can often lead to stunning pictures.

◁ On the day of this shoot it was pouring with rain and I tried to think of a means of creating an unusual picture. I set the camera on a tripod and framed the shot with the car stationary, placing a flashgun on a second tripod. I asked the driver to drive forwards each time he saw the flash fire. Using a shutter speed of one second, the combination of flash and movement created a feeling of speed while keeping the detail sharp on the car's rear.
Audi Quattro, Dartmoor, Devon, England.
Mamiya RB67, 65mm lens, 85B warm-up filter, Metz 60CT-4 flash, Fuji Provia.

The interior of this Lamborghini was very cramped and it was difficult to include enough to make a meaningful picture. In the end I slid to the extreme edge of the passenger seat and held a camera with a wide-angle lens and flashgun, down by my knee and aimed the camera by guesswork.
Lamborghini Countach LP400, near Sant'Agata, Italy. Nikon F3, 20mm lens, Metz 60CT-4 flash, Fuji Provia.

Always keep your eyes open for locations and circumstances that might make for unusual and original images, and try to think laterally about new ways of taking photographs.

All of the techniques described so far can be adapted to suit different circumstances. Remember that the important point with any action picture is to convey the impression of speed, so don't be afraid to use long shutter speeds to impart movement to your pictures. There are many circumstances where, even with a car driven at very low speeds you can create something special by using a little imagination. Try zooming a zoom lens during a long exposure, as this can sometimes create a picture with a real sense of movement.

Study pictures from car magazines (and others) that catch your eye, and try to work out how the photographer took them. Films and television programmes can also be useful sources of inspiration; watch how filmmakers have captured images of moving cars, and think about how and where the camera was positioned. This doesn't mean that you should copy other people's ideas, but think about other ways of employing the techniques and camera angles.

Look out for unusual viewpoints; try climbing on to a wall to gain extra height, or lying on the ground for a distinctive view of the car. Such viewpoints will inevitably be harder to find at motorsport events, but always be ready to look around and exploit any opportunities that exist. When you're out shooting, take every opportunity to experiment and then study your results carefully, making note of what was successful and what needs further work.

Professional photographers often have useful accessories that open up new creative possibilities. Specialist companies serving the motion picture industry manufacture a range of clamps that can be used to attach a camera to a moving car, and while these may be expensive they can be the key to great pictures. Some photographers have constructed elaborate frames that attach to the car and provide unusual viewpoints for driving shots. It is always possible to improvise other ways of doing this but you should always bear in mind that the consequences of a mishap may be damage to the car, the camera or both. Look at the accessories available in camera shops and think of how you might be able to employ them to take unusual car photographs.

Here I used a clamp for attaching a camera to the car window. Intended for use as a substitute tripod, it serves equally well for shooting car interiors. I sat in the rear seat, leaning across to press the shutter. An exposure of ¼ second provided plenty of blur to the hedge outside but as the camera was clamped firmly to the window all the detail on the dashboard is sharp.
Jensen Interceptor, North York Moors, Yorkshire, England. Canon EOS5, 20mm lens, Fuji Velvia.

Motorsport 1

Motorsport is full of fantastic opportunities for great pictures; it's a thrilling spectacle full of colour and excitement that attracts huge global audiences. But the safety measures now in place to protect spectators make it a real challenge to capture images that convey that excitement, and you will have to work hard to achieve successful results.

The first point to make is that enthusiasm for photography and ownership of expensive equipment won't entitle you to any special privileges at major events. At most venues there are barely enough press passes to go around the established media outlets and accredited photographers, and even the keenest amateur simply won't stand a chance of securing one. (In any

◁ It's not necessary to have a press pass to shoot good motorsport pictures. Here the photographer used a long lens from high on a grandstand to fill the frame with this McLaren, and the crowd in the foreground helps to give the picture the atmosphere of a big occasion. Panning with a lens as long as 300mm needs good technique to avoid camera shake. **McLaren MP4 16 at the 2001 Canadian Grand Prix, Montreal, Canada. Canon EOS1v, 300mm lens, Fuji Velvia.**

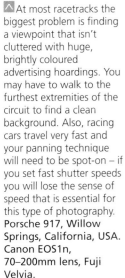

At most racetracks the biggest problem is finding a viewpoint that isn't cluttered with huge, brightly coloured advertising hoardings. You may have to walk to the furthest extremities of the circuit to find a clean background. Also, racing cars travel very fast and your panning technique will need to be spot-on – if you set fast shutter speeds you will lose the sense of speed that is essential for this type of photography. **Porsche 917, Willow Springs, California, USA. Canon EOS1n, 70–200mm lens, Fuji Velvia.**

case, even those photographers lucky enough to secure press passes are often restricted to areas well away from the track.) You will have to compete for the best viewpoints with other spectators, and often this will mean having to use long telephoto lenses.

There are, though, ways of securing the most favourable positions. The first, and most obvious, point is that you should arrive early. Motorsport fans are very devoted, and big races attract huge crowds with the inevitable traffic jams, and often you will have to be out of bed in the small hours to be at the front of the queue for the best spots. At most Grand Prix venues, spectators will camp on or near the circuit for the entire weekend and doing the same will help you avoid the race day mêlée. It helps if you are already familiar with the venue, as you will know the best places to take photographs and can head straight for your preferred spot as soon as the gates open. If you can, walk around the entire circuit well beforehand and identify the best viewpoints.

There are bound to be sections of any circuit that regularly provide dramatic action, and these will always be the best places to aim for. Usually sharp corners make for good pho-

tographs, as the cars' speeds will be lower and they will lean as they turn, but look also for any corners where overtaking manoeuvres are frequently attempted. Often the best place to be at the start of a race is overlooking the first turn, as the scramble after the start to be first through the corner can make for spectacular photographs. Look carefully to see which viewpoints the professionals go for, and think carefully about which direction the light will be falling at different times of the day. Try also to find places where you can avoid the numerous advertising hoardings that adorn most venues and that make for distracting backgrounds.

It can be very worthwhile attending practice sessions as well as (or instead of) races. The same cars will be driving on the same track but there are unlikely to be the same numbers of spectators. Admission is usually much cheaper on practice days, and if you shoot carefully the finished results will probably be indistinguishable from images shot during a race. (Many of the Grand Prix images used in newspapers and magazines are actually shot during practice or qualifying sessions as this makes it easier to meet tight deadlines.)

At any motorsport event it is important to follow the action closely; by continuing to follow this car through the viewfinder after it had passed me I captured an action shot that summed up the nature of the event, with plenty of dust and a good sense of speed. **Rover Metro 6R4, rally course near Silverstone, England. Canon EOS1n, 70–200mm lens, Fuji Provia.**

Motorsport 2

Successful motorsport photography depends on good technique. The cars travel at high speeds and you will have to concentrate hard to get good pictures. While it is tempting to rely on fast shutter speeds to capture the action, this will result in pictures that look like static shots. Practice your panning technique and follow the cars through the viewfinder, taking care to shoot when the action fills the frame. Automatic focusing makes it much easier to keep cars sharp but the high speed of racing cars will be a challenge for even the best systems. Exposure also needs to be spot-on, as you are unlikely to have many chances to get your shot. Learn to recognise situ-

◁ A viewpoint that overlooks the first corner of a circuit is always a good place for shooting action shots. The cars will be jostling for position as they approach after the start, and will be grouped close to each other. You will need to stake your claim to prime vantage points like this early in the day, and a long lens will be necessary to fill the frame with the action.
Touring cars in Rounds 1 and 2, 2001 British Touring Car Championship, Brands Hatch, England. Canon EOS1v, 600mm lens, Fuji Velvia.

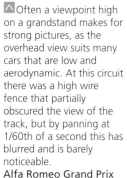

△Often a viewpoint high on a grandstand makes for strong pictures, as the overhead view suits many cars that are low and aerodynamic. At this circuit there was a high wire fence that partially obscured the view of the track, but by panning at 1/60th of a second this has blurred and is barely noticeable.
Alfa Romeo Grand Prix car, Portland International Raceway, Oregon, USA. Canon EOS1n, 300mm lens, Fuji Provia.

ations where the exposure meter could be fooled, and it helps to be thoroughly familiar with your camera's controls so that you can instantly adjust the settings as the need arises.

Most keen motorsport photographers will inevitably want to shoot at major races, such as Grands Prix or the Le Mans 24-hour race. But if you are prepared to lower your sights a little, you may find that the opportunities for good photography are rather better. Every weekend during the summer months there are a multitude of club events, historic races, sprints and one-make series races, every one of which can provide endless possibilities for photography. These events are usually cheap to attend and often have a far more relaxed atmosphere than the highly regulated environment of bigger venues. At some of the smaller events you may be able to secure a photographer's pass that will allow you access to better viewpoints; enquire in advance and be prepared to turn up early to sign the various pieces of paper. (You will need to indemnify the organisers against any claim arising if you're involved in an accident.) You may also have to wear an armband or tabard so that you are clearly identifiable as an accredited photographer. Even if you do manage to secure a pass, you will still only be allowed into certain areas and you must obey any rules or special instructions given.

At most venues, though, you will have to be prepared to shoot from viewpoints accessible to other spectators. This is not necessarily a disadvantage; from high in a grandstand, for example, you can often shoot a car with nothing but track behind it, which provides a clean background and avoids advertising hoardings. You may have a fence between you and the track, but use a long telephoto lens at a wide aperture and this will be invisible on the finished photograph. Get as close as you can to the fence, even pressing your lens up against it if you can. (Panning with a moving car also helps to blur fencing, making it much less prominent on the picture.) In circumstances where you are jostling for position with other spectators, standing on a hard camera case can give the few extra inches of height that make the difference, although you should always act with courtesy to others; you'll make yourself unpopular if you obstruct the view of other paying spectators.

△Small events like this dirt track race offer great opportunities for photography. As it was held on a summer Saturday evening the light was much better than it would have been during the day, and in the relaxed atmosphere no-one objected to me standing up close to the wire fencing to fill the frame with the cars, and to throw the fence out of focus. I used the lens at its maximum aperture and it is hard to tell that the fence is there.
Legends stock car in dirt track race at Banks, Oregon, USA. Canon EOS1n, 70–200mm lens, Fuji Provia.

Motorsport 3

To take successful motorsport pictures you will have to make the most of every opportunity and be prepared for any eventuality. Try to visit as many different viewpoints as you can during the course of a race, and make sure that you shoot cars from a series of different angles. Always be prepared for the action to take an unexpected turn – slides, spins and collisions are all part of

◄ Although the car is only shown in silhouette, this evocative image sums up the atmosphere of the Le Mans 24-hour race perfectly. The photographer chose a viewpoint where he could create a graphic image using the light in the sky after sunset, and then framed the image carefully to include the bridge at the top of the picture. The red lights on the rear of the car helped to break up the silhouette.
Audi R8 at 2001 Le Mans 24-hour race, France. Canon EOS1v, 600mm lens, Fuji Provia.

▲Bad weather can provide an opportunity for unusual pictures. Here a sudden rainstorm made for dramatic racing action, and by shooting from a bridge over the track the photographer was able to frame the shot using the tarmac as the background, which makes it much easier to see the cars clearly.
Touring cars in Rounds 25 and 26 of the 1999 British Touring Car Championship, Silverstone, England. Canon EOS1n, 600mm lens, Fuji Provia.

the spectacle of motorsport and are easy to miss if you're not alert to the possibilities.

Be prepared to move around the circuit in search of the best pictures. Make sure that you can carry all your equipment with you comfortably, and that your bag is packed in such a way that you can quickly lay your hands on an item if required or a fresh roll of film when you need it. Anything you are unlikely to use can be left at home – or locked in the car – to help keep the weight of the bag down, but always make sure that you have plenty of film; that 'shot of a lifetime' might occur on the last lap and there is nothing more frustrating than missing a great picture because you've run out of film. Make sure also that you have spare batteries for cameras, exposure meters and motor drives.

Take advantage of changes in the light to improve your pictures, and pay close attention to the weather forecast and the direction of the sun. On a sunny summer day the light in late afternoon will be much better for photography than the harsh light in the middle of the day, but make sure that by waiting you don't

end up having to shoot into the sun on the best corner. Always keep a few rolls of fast film (as well as a waterproof coat or umbrella) in your bag in case the weather changes unexpectedly, as pouring rain can make for dramatic action shots.

Motorsport photography is not all about frame-filling action shots, it's just as important to capture the essence of the sport. This means always being alert to the creative possibilities of every event; a night shot consisting of blurred headlamp trails might say far more about the Le Mans 24-hour race than a close-up cornering shot of the winning car, and a jubilant pit crew may make a more interesting picture than a car crossing a finishing line. Don't be afraid to make the cars part of an overall view if doing so makes a great picture. And don't forget that the photo opportunities might not all be on the track; keep an eye open for interesting scenes and detail shots in the paddock or the pits. Make sure, too, that you spend at least some time watching the action rather than concentrating solely on taking pictures.

▲Covering an historic rally event, a night section provided the opportunity to take some more abstract pictures. I combined an exposure of half a second with a burst of flash, and the streaked lights provide the sense of movement. A picture like this says more about the atmosphere of an event than a straightforward action shot.
Jaguar Mk X on promenade sprint, Manx Classic, Douglas, Isle of Man. Canon EOS1n, 35mm lens, Metz 60CT-4 flash, Fuji Provia.

Motorsport 4

> For this shot of a Mini Cooper on an historic rally stage, I fitted a wide-angle lens and used the upright format to include some of the surroundings. A close-in shot could have been taken almost anywhere and would have given no idea of the context. I needed to add flash as the light levels in the gorge were poor, and this has had the accidental benefit of catching some of the raindrops, which gives an idea of the conditions the drivers had to contend with.
> **Mini Cooper on Pirelli Classic Marathon, near Cortina, Italy. Nikon F3, 24mm lens, Metz 60CT-4 flash, Fuji Provia.**

> Rather than filling the frame with this Austin-Healey, I chose to include some of the surroundings so that the cloud of dust stirred up by the car created a more atmospheric image. I followed the car around the bend through the viewfinder and shot a sequence of pictures using the motor drive; this was the best one.
> **Austin-Healey 3000 Mk III, rally course at Millbrook Proving Ground, Bedfordshire, England. Nikon F3, 70–200mm lens, Fuji Provia.**

Not all motorsport takes place in the restricted circumstances of the racetrack. Make the effort to visit a rally, a hill-climb or a trial and you will find not only thrilling action but also an environment far more conducive to taking pictures. While there will inevitably be areas that are out-of-bounds for safety reasons, at most of these events you are free to wander the entire length of the course and choose your viewpoint.

To shoot rallying in particular, though, you will have to do your homework and plan carefully. Most rallies run stages in quick succession and you won't be able to get to them all. Decide beforehand which stages will offer the best potential and concentrate on covering those. This is where it really helps to know the locations well; if you know, for example, of a spectacular water-splash or a brow that the cars will leave the ground as they crest, you can make sure you get to the right spot well in advance and be ready as the first car comes through. If you can get hold of route maps in advance, go and check out the best places beforehand but, if you're not on familiar territory, try to ask marshals or other spectators where the best opportunities for photography are to be found.

Remember also that rally fans are a dedicated bunch and will set out for their favourite viewing point well in advance. Traffic jams and parking hassles are inevitable as spectators aim for the most exciting stages. You will need to be up early and to plan your route meticulously, or the action will be over before you've managed to park the car. Most rallies take place during the autumn and winter months, so make sure you wear or take appropriate clothing and footwear, and that your bag of equipment is manageable; some rally stages are long and getting to the best view-points may involve a long hike, followed by a cold wait.

Most rallies feature woodland stages, and this is where flash is likely to be useful. The light in dense woodland is often poor, and by combining a long exposure with a burst of flash you can create some great pictures. Make sure that the car is close enough before you shoot, as flash only has a short range and you will only get one attempt

as each car passes (because the flash will take time to recharge).

While the freedom to wander around and choose your viewpoint is one of the big advantages of a sport like rallying, you must always act responsibly. Every year many spectators are injured through their own stupidity, by standing in places where a car that leaves the road will inevitably end up. Most well-organised rallies employ large numbers of marshals to try to ensure the safety of those watching, but they cannot watch every bend and you should think carefully about the likely consequences of a car leaving the road in the immediate area near where you're standing.

◀ Pictures like this require advance planning and first-class technique. The photographer needed to be familiar with the stage, and had to choose a viewpoint beyond the brow that, as well as giving the opportunity for this type of image, allowed him to work in safety. As each car passed, there was only a split-second to capture the shot as the car flew through the field of view. **Hyundai Accent on 2001 Rally Australia, World Rally Championship. Canon EOS1n, 70–200mm lens, Fuji Velvia.**

Assessing the results

Whether you're shooting action on the road or at the racetrack, it is inevitable that you will end up with many unsuccessful pictures as well as the good ones, and this is where picture editing skills are essential. Look through your finished prints, transparencies or digital images and be prepared to discard any that are technically poor. For this you need to be able to scrutinise your images carefully, and for transparencies or negatives the best way is with a light box and a 'loupe', which is a magnifying glass made for looking at photographs. Digital images will need to be viewed on a high-resolution screen, as the tiny screen on the back of a digital cam-

◄ This is an example of a successful tracking shot. Look carefully at the front of the car and you will see that the radiator grille, the headlamps and the mascot are pin-sharp but the blur in the background gives the sense of movement. This was shot at 1/30th of a second and I used plenty of film to make sure of a sharp result, although the road surface was smooth which helped. I then looked carefully through the results and selected the best images.
Bentley Eight-litre, near Chipping Norton, Oxfordshire, England. Canon EOS1n, 35mm lens, Fuji Velvia.

⌃Driving shots need to convey the impression of speed but at least some of the car should be sharp. Shooting from high on a bank above the road I followed the car through the viewfinder as it drove past, and the result was a sequence of images of different angles of the car, of which only a few were sharp. I chose this one as the car contrasts well with its surroundings.
Maserati A6GCS, near Lake Garda, Italy. Canon EOS1n, 50mm lens, Fuji Velvia.

era doesn't give an image with enough detail for accurate assessment. Start by discarding any images that are significantly under- or over-exposed. Even the most striking action shot is worthless if it's much too dark or too light. If you're shooting on print film you'll need to check the negatives as well, as a print that's incorrectly exposed may be the fault of the machine that produced it.

If the neg looks fine then ask the lab to pro-duce a better print. Similarly, a transparency that is slightly too dark or too light might be rendered usable by getting a print made and asking the lab to make the necessary corrections. Alternatively, by scanning your pictures and manipulating the image with computer software it may be possible to correct small variations in exposure, but in general anything more than a stop or so out might as well go in the bin.

Action photographs need to be sharp on two counts: they must be in focus and at least part of the car should be free of movement or camera shake. In the case of both panning and tracking shots, you are looking for pictures where, as well as being in focus, the car – or some of it – is ren-

dered sharp against a blurred background. This can be a difficult process until you know what to look for. Look carefully at areas of the car con-taining fine detail, and reject any images where no part of the car is sharp. Car number plates are often a good place to look when assessing your pictures, as it is easy to detect sharpness, or the lack of it, when looking at letters and numbers against a contrasting background. Pictures with plenty of blur often work well from an artistic point of view, but there should always be at least a small part of the car that is sharp.

With cornering or similar pictures, you are looking for images where the movement of the car has been 'frozen' by the fast shutter speed and the focus is correct. These pictures always work best if the front of the car is in focus, and again number plates are a useful place to check for this. Images that are out-of-focus are never really successful and should be rejected.

No photographer has a 100 per cent success rate when it comes to action work; the more film you shoot the more successful images you will have, and as your experience increases the better your hit rate will be.

⌃This was taken by pre-focusing the camera, and using this technique a maximum of one sharp shot per 'pass' will be possible. I asked the driver to go through this corner a number of times to increase the chances of success. If you look carefully at the car's number plate you can see that even the small letters below the number are sharp. A shutter speed of 1/250th of a second will usually be sufficient to freeze the movement of a car travelling towards the camera.
BMW M5, near Dungeness, Kent. Nikon F3, 300mm lens, Fuji Provia.

Time of year

For static car photography, it is important to be aware of the light and other conditions that may be encountered at different times of the day and with the different seasons. It is tempting to think that the summer months would be the best time of year to take photographs, but there are several reasons why this is not necessarily the case.

During the summer, the sun is very high in the sky and the light around the middle of the day is very harsh, with bright highlights and dense shadows. These lighting conditions are not ideal for shooting cars, which often look their best in cloudy weather which provides a soft, even light, or with low sunlight. For this reason, many professional car photographers, as well as those who shoot subjects like landscapes, avoid taking photos between the hours of around 10am and 4pm during the summer.

◁ Sunny winter days often provide fantastic light. Here early rain cleared, the sun came out and the light for the whole of a December morning was sensational. It picked out the curves of this Porsche beautifully, and I chose a low viewpoint to hide distracting detail in the background and to exploit the reflection in the puddle. I used a warm-up filter to counter the slightly blue nature of the light, and a graduated grey filter to darken the sky. **Porsche 904/6, test track at Chobham, Surrey, England. Mamiya RB67, 180mm lens, 85A warm-up filter, Fuji Provia.**

△Autumn days often end with great sunsets and a range of colours in the sky. This shot was taken just as the sun was dipping below the horizon, and the tones in the sky have reflected in the car's bodywork and emphasised the elegant curves. To make the most of subtle colours like this, use slow film which has superior colour rendition. It's also important to be ready well before sunset, to have the shot set up in advance and to work quickly.
Jaguar XK140 Roadster, near Denham, Buckinghamshire, England. Mamiya RB67, 90mm lens, graduated grey filter, Fuji Velvia.

By contrast, on a sunny day in winter the low angle of the sun means that lighting conditions can be glorious throughout the day. In summer, 'heat haze' can spoil the clarity of the light, whereas sunny winter days are often crystal clear and this makes for better photographs.

However, the limiting factor in winter is the likelihood of poor weather; sunny days are few and far between and rain, fog and snow all make good photography difficult. On dull winter days, light levels are poor, the light is very flat and pictures taken in these conditions lack contrast and sparkle. Shorter days mean that the time available for photography is limited, and often in winter the roads are wet and muddy, so cars driven even short distances need cleaning before any pictures can be taken. On the other hand, long summer days often mean a very early start is necessary to use the glorious early morning light, or a long wait to shoot at sunset.

Spring and autumn often provide ideal conditions for car photography. Sunny days in spring can have clear light, accompanied by puffy white clouds, while autumn days commonly end with magnificent sunsets. Autumn mornings, when the sun slowly burns off a layer of fog, can result in some spectacular possibilities for photographs, but you will need to work quickly as such conditions never last for long.

As well as understanding the changes to lighting and weather caused by the different seasons, it's important to bear in mind the other changes that occur. In spring, trees and other vegetation often have vivid green colours or colourful blossom, but by the summer the dense leaf cover makes for heavy shadows under trees, and sunny days mean excessive contrast between the light and shady areas of a scene. The golden colours of autumn leaves can make for spectacular backgrounds (especially for red, orange or yellow cars) but barren winter trees make for bleak-looking landscapes, circumstances not helped by the cold blue light of a winter day. Remember, also, that many areas of natural beauty and other good locations are very busy in the summer, but often deserted in winter.

△Landscape changes through the seasons. Fields of oilseed rape provide their characteristic bright yellow colours for a few weeks in the English countryside each spring, and I looked for a location where I could use the colour as a contrast to the blue car. A graduated grey filter helped to retain the deep blue of the sky.
Voisin C28 Aérosport, near Stansted, Essex, England. Mamiya RB67, 65mm lens, graduated grey filter, Fuji Velvia.

Weather

To any photographer shooting outdoors, weather is a constant cause of both joy and frustration. No matter how carefully you plan all the details of a shoot, weather is always the unpredictable factor and can so often mean the difference between great pictures or mundane ones. By listening to TV and radio forecasts, and checking Internet sites, you can usually arm yourself with enough information to be adequately prepared but even with all the modern technology now in place, weather forecasts can never be absolutely relied on. Meteorology is an imprecise science and most forecasters are unwilling to make predictions for more than two or three days ahead, or to be specific about the weather for individual sites.

Most of us think of bright sunshine as ideal

◄ This was taken on a summer day that started bright and sunny, but as soon as we reached the location the clouds rolled in and a persistent drizzle started. The overcast conditions at least ensured that the car was lit evenly, and the red colour helped the car to stand out from the background. I used a polarising filter to reduce the reflection on the car's bonnet and increase the colour saturation.
Alfa Romeo SS 1900, Clee Hill, Shropshire, England. Mamiya RB67, 65mm lens, polarising filter, Fuji Provia.

▲Overcast days replicate the conditions used to photograph cars in the studio. To shoot this elegant Ferrari I deliberately chose a plain background from which the car would stand out. An 81C warm-up filter enhanced the bright yellow of the car and a graduated grey filter darkened the sky.
Ferrari 250 California, Southport beach, Merseyside, England. Mamiya RB67, 65mm lens, 81C and graduated grey filters, Fuji Provia.

conditions for photography, but this isn't always the case when shooting cars. Professional photographers working in studios use soft, even light for car pictures, and overcast conditions produce the same result. Much depends on the colour of the car you're shooting: dark cars can look very drab on dull winter days but colours like red or silver can be shot successfully in almost any weather. Sunshine often creates bright highlights on car bodywork, and during the summer months in particular bright but overcast days often make for better pictures. Changing weather conditions often create the best circumstances for photography; after a shower of rain the air is usually remarkably clear (the rain washes dust particles from the atmosphere) and sunlight will sparkle on wet roads. Conversely an approaching storm can provide a background of threatening clouds which, combined with bright sunshine, will create dramatic pictures.

Rain forces many photographers to pack up and go home. However, cars often look good when covered with raindrops; go in close and make the most of details like badges. Heavy rain makes photography particularly difficult, and

keeping cameras and lenses dry becomes a constant battle. A carrier bag is a useful accessory; place it over the top of the camera to keep the worst of the rain off. High winds cause difficulties, too: on an exposed hillside it can be difficult to avoid camera shake with even a sturdy tripod. Professional photographers often have no choice but to work in bad weather, and most have learnt to make the most of any circumstances to produce good pictures.

Aside from the obvious difficulties of driving in such conditions, it is not easy to take good static car pictures in snow and ice. For good photographs, snow needs to be even and undisturbed, and rarely looks good on anything but a bright sunny day. Roads covered in melting snow and slush are particularly unattractive and cars become filthy very quickly. (Snow causes particular problems for photographers working for car magazines, since long lead times mean that pictures shot during the winter months are often for publication in spring editions.) Mist and fog are also problematic; low contrast levels in the flat light mean that any but the brightest cars will look dull, and backgrounds are obscured.

▲This was a windy day on which heavy showers were followed by sunny spells. Once I'd set this shot up the next squall could be seen approaching and it was important to work quickly before the clouds covered the sun. Because I needed to use a small aperture (for greater depth-of-field), the corresponding long shutter speed has meant that the grass blowing in the breeze has blurred. A graduated grey filter helped to emphasise the dark clouds.
Swallow Doretti (foreground), Triumph TR2, (middle) and Peerless GT (background), near March, Cambridgeshire, England. Mamiya RB67, 50mm lens, Fuji Velvia.

Time of day

On sunny days, it is always best if you can shoot at the beginning or end of the day. The light from the sun when it is low in the sky is much more pleasing, and has a warmer tone that makes for better pictures. Low sunlight also enhances textures and patterns in backgrounds such as build-

◁ Shooting on a clear winter's afternoon, I positioned this MG so that the sun was lighting the side of the car. I also turned the front wheels slightly to catch the light, and although the sun was already a pleasant golden colour I added a warm-up filter to enhance this. At this time of year the light changes very quickly and it is important to be ready to make the most of beautiful light.
MG PA, near Alcester, Warwickshire, England. Mamiya RB67, 65mm lens, 85B warm-up filter, Fuji Velvia.

Each of these three cars was positioned carefully to make the most of the morning sun, and a graduated grey filter enhanced the cumulus clouds in the background. Timing was particularly important at this location, in a scenic village, as it was adjacent to a popular pub and it was important to finish the pictures before cars started arriving at lunchtime and parking in this spot.
Left to right: Riley Roadster, Lea Francis Roadster and Triumph Roadster, Biddestone, Wiltshire, England. Mamiya RB67, 50mm lens, graduated grey filter, Fuji Velvia.

ings or landscapes, and will emphasise the lines and curves of a car. During the summer in particular, most car photographers prefer to work in the early morning or late afternoon. (Look at the car advertisements in magazines and you will see how many are shot at either end of the day.) There are other benefits to working at these times: popular scenic locations are often busy in the middle of the day and by visiting in the early morning or evening you can shoot without the crowds.

The key to good photography is the direction of the light. The instructions given with simple cameras usually suggest that pictures should be taken with the sun behind the photographer's back, but doing so usually results in boring pictures. Light from one side will always make for better results, and this is especially so when the sun is low in the sky. When choosing a location, determine where the sun will be at different times of the day and time your shoot accordingly. If you've chosen to use an interesting building as the backdrop to your picture, make sure you know when the sun will light it to best effect. Work out where shadows at your chosen site will

fall, and bear in mind that tall buildings, or high hills, will obscure the sun at some point in the day. (It's easy, too, to arrive at your chosen location at the appropriate time only to find that the sun creates an obvious shadow of the photographer, the camera and the tripod which encroaches into the picture.)

When it comes to positioning the car, look carefully at the angle of the light before you start. Shooting directly into the light rarely works well with cars; therefore place the subject so that the sun's rays light one side or the front. (You can check with your hand which angle works best before manoeuvring the car into position.) If time allows, shoot at a variety of angles to make the most of the prevailing conditions. Remember that if the sun is just outside the viewfinder when you've composed your shot, lens flare might be a problem and it may help to use a lens hood.

It's not always possible to shoot at ideal times, and often you will have to make the most of the circumstances. Choose your background carefully and watch out for bright highlights that can spoil the look of the car. Fill-in flash, or a reflector, can help to relieve hard shadows.

On a summer morning the light was very harsh, and having positioned the car so that the sun lit the side and the wheels, I added fill-in flash to relieve the deep shadow on the front of the car. I placed the camera close to the hedge (on the left of the frame) so that the eye is led into the picture, and added a graduated grey filter to darken the sky.
MGB, near Maidstone, Kent, England. Mamiya RB67, 65mm lens, graduated grey filter, Broncolor flash, Fuji Velvia.

Sunrise and sunset

The very best times of the day for car photography are around sunrise and sunset. In particular, there is a time that photographers call 'the magic hour' (although it's rarely that long) immediately before the sun rises and just after it sets. The light then is soft and even, but the sky is filled with glorious colours that will reflect in the car's bodywork, highlighting the shape beautifully. This is one of the few occasions when shooting cars against the light works.

◀ The period just after sunset is perfect for car photography. I positioned this Corvette diagonally across the road, as at this angle the light was reflected in the car to best effect. This shot was taken half an hour after the sun had disappeared and light levels were low enough to need a shutter speed of one second. On cold days it's important to watch for condensation forming on car windows after sunset. **Chevrolet Corvette 427, near Effingham, Illinois, USA. Mamiya RB67, 65mm lens, Fuji Provia.**

 On a freezing winter afternoon the sun was fast descending towards the horizon as we arrived at the location. I set up quickly and managed to shoot enough pictures before the sun disappeared, bracketing the exposures widely. A graduated grey filter helped to darken the sky. **MGC, Burton Dassett Hills, Warwickshire, England. Mamiya RB67, 65mm lens, graduated grey and 85A warm-up filters, Fuji Provia.**

Find out the times of sunset and sunrise for the area you're shooting in, and use a compass to work out where in the sky the sun will appear in the morning and set in the evening. A useful gadget called a sun compass will help with this, while a GPS (Global Positioning System) set will give the exact sunrise and sunset times for any location.

It's often the case that dawn and dusk are more spectacular in late autumn and winter than at other times of the year. Certainly the range of colours in the sky will be more impressive. On a clear winter's day the sky after sunset will often be a vivid orange at the horizon, merging with a deep blue higher in the sky. These colours will be at their most impressive in the section of the sky immediately above the point where the sun dipped below the horizon, so you should aim to move the car into a position to exploit this. In summer the tones in the sky at the beginning or end of the day are often rather more muted, largely because heat haze tends to desaturate the vivid colours.

At this time of day the light levels are low despite the colours in the sky and you will need to use a tripod to be sure of sharp results. This also enables the use of slow films, and small apertures for greater depth-of-field. Judging the exposure is tricky; if possible, take a meter reading from an area of the sky away from the brightest part, but always 'bracket' the exposures widely to be sure of a good result. Change the camera settings in half-stop increments when bracketing, if you can, as even half a stop can make a big difference to the end result. The light levels at this time of day change remarkably rapidly and you will need to keep checking the exposure meter. It's also important to check and recheck your focusing, as doing this accurately in low light is not easy.

Shooting when the sun is just above the horizon, at either end of the day, is one of the rare opportunities to include the sun in the picture without the risk of it being much too bright or causing lens flare. However, there are usually only a few minutes when this is possible and it is important to be ready in advance and to work quickly. A graduated grey filter will help to reduce the contrast between a bright sky and the subject.

I had to wait until almost 10pm to get this shot, on an evening in mid-summer, and the last few minutes of sunlight provided the glorious golden light. I positioned the car in such a way that the setting sun and vivid orange sky reflected in the car's front wing and waited until the sun was low enough in the sky. An 85B filter was used to enhance the warm tones. **Alfa Giulia SS, Essex, England. Mamiya RB67, 65mm lens, 85B warm-up filter, Fuji Velvia.**

Shooting at night

Night-time offers a wealth of opportunities to take car pictures, but requires considerable skill on the part of the photographer to overcome the various technical challenges. While there are some situations where the available light will be sufficient for photography, in most cases it will be necessary to use flash and combine this with the ambient light, and this is where care is needed.

Look for locations where there is plenty of street or other lighting in the background, as total darkness around the car rarely makes for successful pictures. It also helps to shoot just before the sky is totally dark, as this helps buildings and hills to stand out against the sky. Wet evenings are particularly good for photography, as lights will reflect in puddles and wet roads.

◄ The purpose of this picture was to show the interior of a Jaguar restored to modern standards. With the camera on a tripod I switched on all the car's interior lights and carefully checked the composition. During an exposure of around one minute, I sat in the back seat of the car and used a powerful torch to add light to the foot wells and seats, to ensure the whole interior was lit evenly. I chose to shoot shortly after sunset to make sure that there was detail in the car's bonnet and the other car would stand out against the sky. **Jaguar Mk II, Clee Hill, Shropshire, England. Mamiya RB67, 50mm lens, Fuji Provia.**

Late at night nobody objected to my putting this Jaguar D-type in an Italian square. I took a light reading with a hand-held meter and based the exposure on this, adding flash from the right-hand side to make sure the car was evenly lit. The exposure was around 30 seconds, and you can see that cars passing have recorded as trails of light. **Jaguar D-type, near Brescia, Italy. Mamiya RB67, 65mm lens, Metz 60CT-4 flash, Fuji Provia.**

The first essential requirement is a good tripod. Even under bright streetlights the light levels are low and you may need to use exposures of 30 seconds or longer. Set the camera on the tripod and frame your shot carefully, taking special care to look for distractions like litter that would be obvious in daylight but difficult to see through a dark viewfinder. Focus carefully; autofocus rarely works reliably in darkness and it may help to switch on the car's headlamps and use them as a check for your focus. Alternatively you can guess (or measure) the distance from the lens to car and set this distance on the focusing ring.

Taking accurate meter readings is difficult, and this is where experimentation comes in handy. Be prepared to take a number of shots at different settings, and don't be afraid to use very long exposures, as the lights of passing cars will appear as attractive trails on the finished photograph. Add flash to retain detail in the car, and again experiment with various settings. During a long exposure you can even run around and fire the flash several times in different places. You could also try experimenting

with torches or other portable lamps.

Some forms of artificial lighting will create a colour cast on film. You could consider using film balanced for tungsten lights but this makes it difficult to add flash (as flash is balanced for daylight film). In any case, few street or neon lights are compatible exactly with tungsten film. Car photographs taken at night are usually improved by switching on the headlamps and hazard flashers, but be careful not to flatten the car's battery by doing so. (You'll need to switch off the engine, as the vibration of the car as it ticks over will cause it to blur during a long exposure.)

Shooting at night has the added advantage that it may permit the use of locations and backgrounds that would be too busy during the day. City centres are usually brightly lit, with plenty of neon signs and passing traffic, and parking restrictions that would prevent photography during the day are usually suspended overnight. Shooting late at night often allows you to put a car in places where you would be quickly hustled off during the day, but be prepared to work quickly.

In central London I parked this Mazda in a busy side street without the risk of a parking ticket, as restrictions only apply until 6.30pm. The exposure was around 30 seconds at f/8, and I fired a flashgun from inside a doorway to the right of the car to add light to the side of the car and the wheels. Again passing traffic has created trails of light, which add to the picture. **Mazda MX-5, central London, England. Mamiya RB67, 50mm lens, Metz 60CT-4 flash, Fuji Provia.**

Choosing locations 1

The big advantage of cars as subjects for photography is that they can be easily moved to almost any choice of location. You can choose the most appropriate setting for the car and time your shoot to suit weather and lighting conditions. Settings that make for good photographs in themselves often make good locations for car shoots. Beautiful landscapes, impressive or historic buildings, coastline, rivers, lakes, hills or mountains can all make great backgrounds for car pictures. But it is important to choose a location that is appropriate to the car, and to avoid obvious colour clashes. It always helps to reconnoitre locations in advance; this saves time, keeps mileages down and avoids getting the car excessively dirty between leaving home and taking pictures.

◁ This shot of a Lamborghini was taken in London's Docklands area, and I looked for somewhere to park the car that had room for me to set up portable lights as well as the camera. I chose a viewpoint that would have the office blocks as the background, and started shooting while there was still some light in the sky so that the buildings would stand out. The water in the foreground was hauled out of an adjacent dock by a helper and poured across the road to create a reflection.
Lamborghini Diablo SV, near Canary Wharf, London, England. Mamiya RB67, 65mm lens, Broncolor portable flash, Fuji Provia.

▲This Aston Martin had been used in the James Bond film *GoldenEye,* and this disused airship hangar was chosen as a location because of its resemblance to some of the spectacular sets used in Bond films. Light levels inside the hangar were low and the daylight filtering through the windows on the far side has over-exposed slightly, while the holes in the roof have given the impression of a starlit sky. **Aston Martin DB5, airship hangar at Cardington, Bedfordshire, England. Mamiya RB67, 50mm lens, Fuji Provia.**

Built-up areas are an obvious choice of location, but finding good spots can be difficult. In places where there are parking restrictions or too many other cars, consider returning at a quiet time, such as early on a Sunday morning. Avoid locations where there are distracting road signs or street furniture, or excessive litter. As long as you are legally parked there will normally be no restriction on photography in most towns and cities, and you have every right to take pictures from public areas such as pavements, so anyone who objects to you using their house, shop front or office as a background (or asks for payment) probably has no right to do so. However, it is courteous to ask and most people will have no objection. If you intend to use a private forecourt or car park as a location you will certainly need to ask for permission and sometimes a location fee will be asked. Beware that in many countries it is illegal to photograph post offices and banks (for security reasons) and many government offices or military buildings will also be out-of-bounds (and you may get yourself arrested for taking pictures of such places).

Most buildings that have architectural interest will make good backgrounds. Modern hi-tech buildings make good backgrounds for some cars, while pretty villages may work well for classic or vintage cars. But avoid obvious clichés (such as using a stately home as a backdrop for a Bentley); too many of these ideas have been overused, and it's better to look for a fresh approach. Many historic houses and castles are frequently in demand for photo and film shoots, and will be well versed in exploiting the commercial possibilities. They usually have set fees that are way beyond what any amateur photographer (and most magazines) can afford and you may have to set your sights on more mundane surroundings. Many private houses with large grounds will also be aware of the possibility for charging location fees, but it's always worth asking (politely). Smart hotels or country clubs may be more amenable, particularly if you offer them some of the resulting images, but always remember that their priority will be serving their clientele and they are unlikely to go to great lengths to help you. You will certainly make yourself unpopular if you cause an obstruction or drive on to carefully tended lawns in the pursuit of pictures.

▲A scenic village, complete with thatched cottages, was a good location for these two classic cars. The viewpoint was carefully chosen to avoid other cars parked nearby and to crop out various road signs, and I added a warm-up filter to counteract the cold tones of a winter day. **Wolseley Eight (foreground) and Morris Eight, near Hallaton, Leicestershire, England. Mamiya RB67, 65mm lens, 85B warm-up filter, Fuji Velvia.**

Choosing locations 2

In general, rural locations pose far fewer problems for the car photographer than built-up areas. You can usually find plenty of space in the countryside and in most places there are few restrictions on parking cars. Detailed maps make location hunting much easier, and you should mark likely places carefully for future reference.

Many photographers favour areas where there are hills and mountains, as you can shoot from the valley floor looking towards distant peaks, or from the hillside looking down. Mountains often have rocky outcrops or steep drops that make great settings for car pictures. Open moorland can be used for pictures with clean, uncluttered backgrounds, but look for iso-

lated trees or rocks that can be used to add interest to a foreground or to a blank sky. Forests sometimes work well but remember that dense woodland will block much of the available light, and that trees will provide a dark background that may not work with dark cars. Look also for sites adjoining water; lakes and rivers often make good backgrounds, especially in calm weather when they can be used to create pictures with reflections. At sunset or sunrise water will reflect the colours in the sky, which can make for great photographs.

The sea also works well, and often you can find a sea front or slipway where you can shoot with a background of breaking waves. Beach

◀ High on a Welsh hillside (and just a short distance from a café and a full car park) I found this heap of slate waste with texture that provided a good contrast to the sleek lines of this Honda NSX. I positioned the car carefully to make best use of the light, and by using a very low viewpoint I was able to virtually fill the background with the waste heap. A telephoto lens, used at a wide aperture, kept the foreground and background out-of-focus but the car sharp.
Honda NSX, near Llangollen, North Wales. Mamiya RB67, 180mm lens, Fuji Provia.

tend to use rather spurious means of deciding what constitutes an amateur photographer and you may find yourself classed as a professional just because your camera is on a tripod. Anyone shooting landscapes is unlikely to be troubled but using a car as a subject tends to attract attention from rangers or wardens and you may be asked to pay a location fee. Unless you are shooting for a paying client it is worth arguing the case, as such fees exist to prevent commercial enterprises from exploiting areas of natural beauty for profit and not to restrict members of the public out to enjoy (or photograph) the scenery. If you're not sure, ask in advance about any rules and bye-laws that apply to photography.

∨Mountains always make great photographs; here the snow-capped peaks made a much better background for the interior of this Ferrari than a flat landscape would have done. The low sunlight on a summer's evening picked out the ridges and gave the rock a warm tone. I used a tripod to make sure of enough depth-of-field.
Ferrari 166M, Col des Mosses, near Lausanne, Switzerland. Nikon F3, 24mm lens, 81A filter, Fuji Provia.

∧It's always worth looking for locations where you can get up high and look down over landscapes. Although it was overcast the views from near the top of this Italian hillside were spectacular and I climbed up on a bank above the car to create this composition. The bright red car was a good contrast with the greenery, and I used a graduated grey filter to retain detail in the distant hills.
Lancia Flaminia Sport, near Montecatini Terme, Italy. Mamiya RB67, 65mm lens, graduated grey filter, Fuji Velvia.

huts, lighthouses, fishing or sailing boats and piers are other possibilities at the coast. There are many beautiful parts of the countryside or the coast which are popular with tourists and day-trippers, and if you try to shoot at busy times you'll be in competition with others for the best viewpoints, and plagued by other people (and their vehicles) creating distracting backgrounds. Therefore, shoot out of season, or at times of the day when no-one else is around.

Always remember that large areas of the countryside are used for agriculture, and that you should not trespass on private property, or damage crops, in the course of taking pictures. If your chosen location is not on land with rights of public access, find out who the landowner is and ask for permission. Thoughtless actions by a few people have led, in many places, to barriers, fences and locked gates being used to prevent access to areas that were previously open. This is a great shame and irresponsible actions can only lead to increased restrictions.

Some national or country parks have rules about commercial photography but are usually more relaxed about amateurs. Unfortunately, they

Choosing locations 3

The sharp-eyed car photographer will always be on the hunt for locations and circumstances that make for good pictures. Many places suggest themselves, through being inherently photogenic with or without the addition of a car. (And there are some truly beautiful cars that photograph well almost anywhere.) But if you want to create something special, look for unusual and distinctive settings. Sometimes you may spot potential locations in magazines or on television programmes; make a note of the details and try to find out if access is possible with a car. Often the

◁ Out looking for locations, I spotted a railway siding used by a steam railway for storing rolling stock awaiting restoration. I contacted the railway's offices and explained what I wanted to do and permission for the shoot was granted in return for a donation. The rusty carriages contrasted well with the sleek lines of the Ferrari, and I chose to shoot at a time when the sun would light the scene evenly. Limited space meant that I had to shoot pressed against a fence at the edge of the yard. **Ferrari Mondial qv, railway yard near Tenterden, Kent, England. Mamiya RB67, 90mm lens, Fuji Velvia.**

Dungeness in Kent was selected for this shot because, by careful choice of viewpoint, it could be made to resemble the American mid-west. The telegraph poles, leaning sign and deep blue sky helped to create the appropriate mood. The area is part of a private estate and its popularity with photographers has led to the levying of location fees for commercial work.
Chevrolet Impala, Dungeness, Kent, England. Mamiya RB67, 50mm lens, graduated grey filter, Fuji Velvia.

best images come from thinking laterally, and this applies as much to location hunting as to any other aspect of photography.

Rather than thinking where you could put a car, start by thinking of all the places where you *couldn't* put a car. Then try to work out ways of overcoming the difficulties. Sometimes this will simply be a case of asking for permission, but in other circumstances actually gaining access with a car may be a difficulty. Often the best locations are those places where cars wouldn't normally go, such as quarries or beaches, and as long as you are not trespassing and can gain access without damaging the car, then don't be afraid to use unconventional settings. (Beware of the potential pitfalls, though: more than one photographer has had to hastily seek assistance after getting a car stuck on a beach with a rising tide. Another managed to drive a car off a jetty while trying to position it for a photograph.)

Keep an eye open for locations where you can use unusual viewpoints, such as looking down on the car from above, and for places where there are interesting colours, or combinations of colours, that work as backgrounds. Interesting

architectural details can make good settings. Sometimes derelict buildings or factories make great locations; rusty metal doors or peeling paint make good backgrounds to pristine cars. Scrap yards, abandoned cars or farm machinery can sometimes provide interesting contrasts. Occasionally, something as seemingly mundane as a pile of old tyres or felled trees can be used to good effect, and being able to spot the potential of unlikely settings is one of the skills that the creative photographer needs. Sometimes locations that are uninspiring by day are completely different at night; look for interesting neon signs or buildings with distinctive lighting. Some locations change completely at different times of the year; for example, you could try shooting at the seaside in the depths of winter.

Look out also for locations that work for particular cars. An American 'themed' restaurant might work with a huge American car, and the front of a trendy shop might suit a chic Italian sports car. Think about using industrial or heritage museums, as sometimes these can be used to find appropriate 'period' backgrounds for historic cars.

This spot, on a beach in the Bahamas, was only just off a road and it was easy to place this Siata without the risk of it getting stuck. The red car made a good contrast to the sand and the blue-green sea, and the overcast conditions helped as on a sunny day there would have been too much contrast between the open beach and the shade under the trees.
Siata 200CS, near Nassau, Bahamas. Mamiya RB67, 65mm lens, Fuji Provia.

Exposure for static photography

> All three of these pictures are acceptable, and choosing between them is largely down to personal preference. In circumstances like these, when the shot is effectively unrepeatable, film is the cheapest part of the whole exercise and a few extra frames to be sure of a good result – and to provide a selection of usable alternatives – are easy to justify. **Lamborghini Countach LP400 (foreground) and Ferrari Berlinetta Boxer, airfield near Kemble, Gloucestershire, England. Mamiya RB67, 65mm lens, graduated grey filter, Fuji Velvia.**

When photographing stationary cars, there is far more time available to take exposure readings and adjust camera settings than when shooting action pictures. Nevertheless, it's important to be aware of the various situations that can make judging exposure tricky, and to know how to deal with them.

The big advantage when shooting static images is that there is time to 'bracket' exposures and this is the key to guaranteeing good results. Bracketing means shooting a sequence of pictures either side of the 'correct' exposure, deliberately under- and over-exposing those additional pictures. This way, if your camera's exposure meter has been fooled by the situation you are almost certain to still have a usable picture. But even with an exposure meter that is totally reliable, there is still a good reason to bracket, particularly when shooting in low light or unusual conditions such as at dawn or dusk. The fact is that, in these circumstances, there is no such as thing as correct exposure. You could shoot a sequence of half a dozen exposures, all at different settings, and every one might be usable. Show those pictures to several photographers and each might choose a different one as the 'correct' exposure. The darker pictures may be rich, moody images while the lighter ones might show the detail better in the car.

In theory, under identical lighting conditions, a black car and a white car should require exactly the same exposure. In reality this is rarely the case: a dark-coloured car will always need an extra stop or half-stop of exposure or it will possibly end up too dark on the finished photograph. Conversely, white or very light cars are easily prone to being over-exposed and sometimes it is necessary to decrease the indicated exposure by half a stop to preserve tone in the car's body and prevent it appearing 'bleached out'. This is especially the case in bright sunshine. Experienced photographers will soon recognise circumstances like these but even so, most will bracket exposures to be sure.

The tolerance of transparency film to under- or over-exposure is much less than that of print films, and for this reason most professional pho-

> This was a situation that even the best exposure meter would have struggled to cope with. There was a difference of four stops in the readings taken from the sunshine in front of the house and from the shadow beside the nearest car. This is approaching the limit of transparency film's ability to handle extremes of contrast and judging the best compromise was essential: if the picture was too dark the cars in the shade would have disappeared, too light and the brickwork would have bleached out. I set an exposure midway between the two readings and bracketed widely to guarantee an acceptable result. **Front to back: Austin-Healey 100, Triumph TR2, Jowett Jupiter, and Morgan Plus 4, Hedingham Castle, Essex, England. Mamiya RB67, 65mm lens, Fuji Velvia.**

tographers using transparencies will bracket, in half-stop increments, a stop or more either side of the indicated exposure. With print films it is only necessary to bracket one full stop either side of the recommended setting, but in tricky lighting conditions or with an unrepeatable shot it is worth bracketing more widely.

Digital camera users have the luxury of being able to view the saved image on the screen on the back of the camera to check the exposure but it is still worth shooting a few at different settings, as, for example, lost shadow or highlight detail may not be immediately apparent on the small, low-res image. There are other good reasons for shooting additional frames when using film; typically if a scratch or a processing mark appears it will be on what would otherwise have been the best shot from the session, so a few extra frames at the time of the shoot saves the expense, hassle and compromised image quality that results from having duplicates of favourite photographs made later. When you've gone to a lot of trouble to set up a shoot and the light is perfect, the incidental expense of a few extra frames is worthwhile.

Composition 1

Put very simply, composition is the art of placing the various elements of a photograph in the viewfinder until a pleasing arrangement is achieved. While it is relatively easy to explain and understand the technical aspects of photography, composition is very subjective and the ability to do it well is acquired rather than learnt. The best way to improve your composition skills is to take photographs and analyse them carefully, trying to work out how they could have been improved. Look at photographs in books and magazines that you particularly like, and ask

◄ This image is composed along the 'thirds' principle, although when I was setting up the camera I didn't consciously follow the rule – this is simply the arrangement I ended up with that looked best. I placed the camera low down on the tripod to make the most of the metal poles and chains in the foreground, and using a telephoto lens the limited depth-of-field ensures that the viewer's eye is 'led' to the car. I also had to be careful that the boat on the mud flats didn't appear to be sitting on the car's bonnet, which it might have done had I moved the camera slightly to the right.
Ferrari 500 Superfast, near Chichester, West Sussex, England. Mamiya RB67, 180mm lens, Fuji Provia.

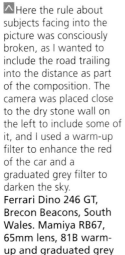

⌃Here the rule about subjects facing into the picture was consciously broken, as I wanted to include the road trailing into the distance as part of the composition. The camera was placed close to the dry stone wall on the left to include some of it, and I used a warm-up filter to enhance the red of the car and a graduated grey filter to darken the sky.
Ferrari Dino 246 GT, Brecon Beacons, South Wales. Mamiya RB67, 65mm lens, 81B warm-up and graduated grey filters, Fuji Provia.

yourself how the photographer came to compose the picture in that way. There are, though, some basic 'rules' of composition that, although they need not be slavishly followed, form a good basis for photography.

The first, and most widely known, is the 'rule of thirds'. This states that the best position for a subject in the frame is either one-third of the way across the frame (from either side) or one-third of the way up or down the frame. The logical conclusion of this is that the very best position for a subject – such as a car – is at the intersection of the thirds. That is, the four points within the frame where a series of lines dividing the image in three, horizontally and vertically, would intersect. Look at a range of photographs – and paintings or drawings – and you will notice how often this rule is used to make strong images.

Taking the rule of thirds a step further, we end up with a series of 'don'ts'. Avoid placing your main subject close to the edge of the frame, and images where the focal point of the picture is in the dead centre of the frame are rarely successful. Similarly when you are shooting, say, a car in a landscape the horizon should ideally be one-third of the way up or down the frame, but often

it is better to adjust the camera until what you see in the viewfinder looks 'right'.

Another rule of composition that is often taught is that subjects should face 'into' the picture rather than 'out' of it. In general this is a good guideline but you will often find, when it comes to shooting cars, that it is a rule that can be ignored when the subject suits an alternative arrangement. If in doubt, try two versions of the shot – when taking static pictures there is often time to shoot a car in several different compositional arrangements and then make a final selection from the results.

Other aspects of composition are really common sense: look carefully through your viewfinder and try to identify any potentially distracting elements. Remember that you are viewing in three dimensions a subject that will be represented in two dimensions on a photograph, and that an innocuous-looking telegraph pole in the distance may appear on the final image to be growing out of the car's roof. Things like this are a frequent cause of spoiled pictures. Look carefully also for discarded litter; even something as small as a cigarette end that is hard to see through the viewfinder will be the first thing you notice on the resulting picture.

⌃Contrasting a car with other elements in a scene can sometimes create interesting pictures. Here I chose to emphasise the shape of the fishing boat by reducing it almost to a silhouette, and added a burst of flash to pick out the rear of the car.
BMW M5, Dungeness, Kent. Mamiya RB67, 90mm lens, graduated grey filter, Metz 60CT-4 flash, Fuji Provia.

Composition 2

Skilled photographers will always look for an unusual angle or viewpoint to enhance their pictures, and before unpacking your camera it is a good idea to consider all the different ways of composing your shot. Creative photography is all about making the most of any situation, and there are some compositional techniques that can be used to make striking images out of ordinary circumstances.

Look for lines or shapes in your surroundings that echo the outline of the car, and position the car in such a way that the similarity is clear. Always watch for opportunities to exploit reflections, as these can be used to good effect; park a car next to a pool of water – or even a puddle – and shoot from low down, and it is possible to create a striking symmetrical image. And don't be afraid to tilt your camera, as strong diagonal lines create an impression of movement in photographs that often works well.

When positioning your camera and the car, try to exploit anything that can be used to create an

◁ In this French village, the pretty *mairie* was conveniently close to this arch. After positioning the car, I moved back and framed the shot with a telephoto lens. The arch had the added advantage that it enabled me to crop out other parked cars that would have been a distraction, and whose owners would have been difficult to trace in a busy village. The backlight on the hanging flowers was a coincidental benefit.
Citroën Traction Avant 15-Six, Monpazier, Dordogne, France. Mamiya RB67, 180mm lens, Fuji Provia.

lens, the distance from the camera position to the frame and the distance from the frame to the subject are all crucial. You may need to spend some time moving the car, moving the camera and changing lenses before achieving a pleasing arrangement. Using a wide-angle lens you may end up with a car that is too small in the viewfinder, but fit a telephoto and it will be difficult to include any of the 'frame' you are shooting through unless you have plenty of room to move back. The finished result will always work better if you use a wide aperture to limit the depth-of-field as this will concentrate the eye of the viewer on the car. This is, after all, how our eyes work – by focusing on one thing at a time.

⊠I deliberately placed the camera behind this boat to create some foreground interest in this picture; the alternative would have been the rather dull mud flat. A telephoto lens and wide aperture gave the narrow depth-of-field that means the eye is led straight to the car.
BMW CSL 'Batmobile', Sheringham, Norfolk, England. Mamiya RB67, 180mm lens, Fuji Provia.

⌃Having spotted the potential of this fence, it was simply a case of positioning the cars carefully to create this composition. The gate lying on the ground – already there when I arrived – was moved slightly to make a more pleasing arrangement. The combination of low winter sunlight and a warm-up filter provided the rich warm tones.
BMW 2002 Turbo, Saab 99 Turbo and Renault 18 Turbo, near Lichfield, Staffordshire, England. Mamiya RB67, 65mm lens, 85B warm-up and graduated grey filters, Fuji Velvia.

interesting foreground, in particular, to lead the viewer's eye into the picture. Placing the camera close to something in the foreground and deliberately leaving it out-of-focus is an established compositional trick that takes the eye straight to the subject, and there are endless possibilities for variations on this. Try placing your camera immediately behind a tree or a lamppost and focusing on the car, as though the viewer is peeping from behind the object. (Notice how often this technique is used in cinematography, to concentrate the viewer's eye on action taking place away from the camera.) Alternatively you can move objects in the scene into a position directly in front of the camera to achieve the same effect. Try moving back with a telephoto lens, or using a wide aperture so that the depth-of-field is limited; this way the subject stands out from its surroundings.

Another well-used technique that is still effective is to shoot the subject through a frame of some sort. This could be an arch, a doorway, a window or even a hole in a fence, but on many occasions it makes for interesting pictures in otherwise mundane situations. Always be on the lookout for opportunities to use this neat compositional trick. To make it work well, the choice of

Using depth-of-field

While shutter speed and aperture combine to give correct exposure, both affect other aspects of the picture and the creative photographer can exploit these to good effect. The lens aperture controls the depth-of-field in the finished image; that is, the amount of the subject in front of, and behind, the point of focus that will appear sharp. This is a valuable creative tool and it is important to understand how to use it in order to achieve the result you are after. A shot of a car in a dramatic landscape will be significantly improved by pin-sharpness that extends from

For this detail shot I used a telephoto lens and set the maximum aperture of f/2.8, to ensure that the background was completely out-of-focus. This also meant that I was using a fast shutter speed, which enabled me to safely hand-hold the camera.
Bentley mascot, Canon EOS1n, 70–200mm lens, Fuji Velvia.

just in front of the camera to the distant horizon, while a close-up of an interesting detail will benefit from a background that is completely out-of-focus. Small lens apertures give greater depth-of-field than wide ones, and you should always be aware of the effect that changing the aperture will make to the sharpness of your picture. Telephoto lenses have inherently less depth-of-field than wide-angle lenses so always choose your lens carefully with this in mind.

If you want the sharpness in your picture to extend from front to back you will need to choose a standard or wide-angle lens and set an aperture of around f/16 or f/22. This will often make it necessary to place the camera on a tripod, to allow the use of the correspondingly long shutter speed (alternatively use fast film). Some cameras have a depth-of-field preview facility that temporarily stops the lens down so that you can see the effect of the chosen aperture, but at small apertures the viewfinder will be very dark and it is difficult to judge the focus accurately. More useful is the depth-of-field scale featured on most lenses, which allows you to read off the distances either side of your

point of focus that will be sharp. The depth-of-field scale also allows you to use something called the 'hyperfocal distance' to maximise sharpness. Depth-of-field extends further behind the point of focus than towards the camera, and by looking carefully at the scale on the lens you can adjust the focus to exploit the full extent of the depth-of-field for your chosen aperture. This is a technique worth becoming familiar with.

There are many situations where it is important to minimise the depth-of-field, for example to throw a distracting background out of focus, or to concentrate the viewer's attention on the subject. For this you should choose a telephoto lens and set the lens's maximum aperture (typically f/2 or f/2.8). On a sunny day this may not be possible, as your camera may not have a sufficiently fast shutter speed to allow the use of the widest aperture. You could consider switching to a slower film, or fit a neutral density or polarising filter to reduce the amount of light entering the lens. You will need to take special care with your focusing, as at wide apertures the slightest slip will result in a picture that isn't sharp.

For this picture I wanted the entire car to be sharp, and to retain detail in the background landscape. Working with the camera on a tripod, I set an aperture of f/16 and, with the threatening dark clouds reducing the light still further, I needed an exposure of around ½ a second. A graduated grey filter emphasised the dark sky.
Alfa Romeo 2900B, near Crickhowell, South Wales. Mamiya RB67, 65mm lens, Fuji Velvia.

Here it was important to keep the depth-of-field to a minimum, as I wanted the natural L-shape created by the breakwater to lead the eye into the picture and the car to be the focal point. In the sunshine the maximum aperture of f/4.5 meant that I needed to use 1/400th of a second, the fastest available on the Mamiya camera.
Rover P5 'Cyclops', Herne Bay, Kent, England. Mamiya RB67, 180mm lens, Fuji Provia.

Using shutter speed

There will be many occasions when it is possible to use shutter speed as a creative tool to improve your pictures. Just as, when shooting action pictures, shutter speed can be used to make the difference between an ordinary picture and one that has a good sense of speed, it can liven up static pictures. In particular there are numerous circumstances when a long shutter speed can be used to blur anything in the scene that is moving, and it is always worth keeping an eye open for opportunities to do this.

Streams and waterfalls, breaking waves, trees or flags moving in the breeze, or other vehicles passing by can all be blurred in this way and will give your pictures a sense of energy and movement. On a windy day you can use a long shutter speed to blur clouds that are being blown across the sky. There may also be occasions when you can use a long shutter speed to remove distracting elements from a scene. An example might be a situation where passers-by keep wandering across the background of your shot; by using an exposure of around one second, anyone moving through the scene will be virtually invisible on the

Here I had chosen the slipway as a location that would suit the car, and decided to make the most of the breaking waves in the background by using a shutter speed of ½ a second. Even in the overcast conditions this meant using a polarising filter to reduce the light sufficiently. I waited for a wave to break before releasing the shutter each time. Using locations like this requires care, as a mishap can result in the car ending up in the sea! **Nardi Alfa, near Nassau, Bahamas. Mamiya RB67, 90mm lens, polarising filter, Fuji Provia.**

speeds longer than around one second is 'reciprocity failure'. This occurs because film is manufactured to be used under normal lighting conditions, and does not display the same sensitivity when used with very long exposures. The effect can lead to under-exposed pictures and to odd colour casts. Film manufacturers usually publish details of the degree of exposure and colour correction necessary with each film under different circumstances, but if you do not have the necessary information to hand you should bracket widely. This is another good reason to stick with a film that you particularly like, as you will learn to recognise situations where reciprocity failure is likely to occur, and correct accordingly.

On a windy afternoon I noticed the movement in the tree and decided that it would work as a feature of the picture. I composed the picture as an upright shot, and needed to use an 8x neutral density filter – which reduces the light entering the lens by three stops – to allow me to use an exposure of one second.
Gordon-Keeble IT, near Romford, Essex, England. Mamiya RB67, 90mm lens, 8x neutral density filter, Fuji Velvia.

Having set this picture up using the beach huts as part of the composition, I moved the deck chair carefully into the right place in the shot and waited for passers-by. An exposure of ¼ of a second meant that they blurred enough to give a sense of movement; if I had used a slower shutter speed they would have almost disappeared.
Panther Solo, Bournemouth seafront, Dorset, England. Mamiya RB67, 180mm lens, Fuji Provia.

final image. Similarly, working in a busy city location, you could use a long shutter speed to turn background traffic into a colourful blur.

It is necessary to use a tripod when using long shutter speeds to avoid the picture being spoiled by camera shake. Use a cable release as well, just to make sure that the action of your finger on the shutter button doesn't induce any movement, and some cameras have the facility to lock the mirror up in advance of releasing the shutter, to prevent vibration. Using long shutter speeds often means setting the smallest aperture on your lens, but in bright sunshine even this may not give a long enough exposure for the effect you are trying to achieve; again, slower film or filters may solve the problem.

Long shutter speeds are often essential when shooting in low light, but always be aware of the creative potential on offer; an exposure of several minutes will render passing headlamps as 'trails' of light and there may well be some locations where you can use a long exposure to produce an interesting effect on moving water when shooting at dawn or dusk.

One thing to be aware of when using shutter

Making the most of the location 1

Creative photography is all about careful observation. Before even looking through the camera,
it is well worth taking the time to thoroughly
explore your chosen location and decide on all
the different aspects of it that might contribute
to good pictures. The obvious viewpoint that

◁ This is a location that many car photographers have used, and it is always a challenge to find new ways of using familiar spots. Here the winter sunlight created interesting patterns of light and shade on the hillside and I positioned the cars so that they would catch the sun but also so that their shapes would work well with the curves and lines of the hillside. I originally chose to shoot from much closer in but then moved back to use the area of shade in front of the camera as part of the composition.
Ferrari 400i (foreground) and Lamborghini Espada, Burton Dassett Hills, Warwickshire, England. Mamiya RB67, 90mm lens, Fuji Velvia.

Using a country house location, I wandered around and found this viewpoint, up a series of steps, that enabled me to use this arch as a frame and to get a clear view of the car largely free of distractions. As it was an overcast day I positioned the car carefully to make the most of the light, and used a warm-up filter to counter the prevailing cool mood of the scene.
Lancia Appia Series 2, near Oxford, England. Mamiya RB67, 65mm lens, 85B warm-up filter, Fuji Provia.

suggests itself as soon as you arrive rarely turns out to be the best one; wander around and consider all the features of the location that you might be able to include in your pictures. Look for viewpoints that make best use of the site, and always aim for simple compositions and for clean, uncluttered backgrounds. Pay particular attention to any details that might spoil the picture and work out how you can avoid including them; sometimes by careful choice of viewpoint you can conceal potential distractions. Don't be afraid to move things around to improve your picture, but always make sure that you leave things as you found them and avoid causing damage.

It is always the case at well-known beauty spots or scenic viewpoints that there is one place that everyone uses to take their pictures, but professional photographers will always look for interesting alternatives. Anything that you can use to make your pictures original and distinctive should be considered. Avoid shooting everything with the camera at eye-level, as sometimes using a higher or lower viewpoint makes for a better picture. Consider lying on the ground or climbing

on to a wall – or even a tree – if doing so makes for a better picture, and look for staircases or fire escapes that might offer alternative viewpoints. Keep an eye open for shapes and lines that could be used as part of a strong composition, and look also for areas of colour or texture that might complement or contrast with the car you're shooting.

Once you start shooting, it is very often the case that your pictures improve as the session goes on. As you 'warm-up' and become more attuned to composing pictures you will start to notice more alternative options. Once you have taken the trouble to set up a shoot, it is worth shooting as much film as necessary to get the best possible result, but beware of shooting lots of pictures indiscriminately. It's much better to concentrate hard on creating a few strong images, and you should make sure before pressing the shutter that you are entirely happy with what you have in the viewfinder. Don't settle for using one camera and lens combination; each time you move the car or change your position, try changing lenses and see which makes the strongest picture.

The empty beach made a rather uninspiring location, so I chose to use this line of posts as part of the composition. The car was positioned carefully so that it was clearly visible between the two posts nearest the camera, but care had to be taken to avoid making obvious tyre marks in the sand in the foreground.
Alfa Romeo 2000 Berlina, Weston-super-Mare, Somerset, England. Mamiya RB67, 65mm lens, Fuji Velvia.

Making the most of the location 2

When shooting cars, it is often tempting to go in close and fill the frame with the subject. There are undoubtedly cars that suit this approach, but there are occasions when it is appropriate to include more of the surroundings and show the car in context. This helps to create a mood and if you are working in a beautiful or distinctive set-

ting it is better to make it part of your picture.

Think of car pictures as landscape images of which the car is a part. Look for opportunities to include cars as part of a scene rather than as the sole subject. Choose locations that can be used with a car to create a certain atmosphere: there are many places where you can use a beautiful

◁ Shooting in a quiet Italian lane, I had done some pictures of this car from close in but then spotted the potential for this image, in which the car is included as part of the surroundings. The camera and tripod were placed up a steep bank, and this higher viewpoint helped me to include the road as part of the composition. The bright red car stood out well amongst the bare trees. **Lancia A6GCS, near Lake Garda, Italy. Mamiya RB67, 90mm lens, polarising filter, Fuji Velvia.**

locations within a relatively small area. They quickly need to identify the potential of settings that are less than ideal, and many of the best pictures in car magazines are done in locations that most photographers wouldn't pause to consider. By studying such pictures carefully, you can often identify the factors that led the photographer to choose a particular viewpoint, or the elements in the scene that have been included (or excluded) to improve the image.

Always remember that as well as finding the best viewpoint, it is important to make best use of the prevailing lighting conditions; be prepared to change your original ideas if sudden changes in the weather or the light make an alternative approach preferable. Try to use the car, the location and the light in combination to make good pictures. Work out the time of day that best suits the chosen location and time your visit accordingly. If you can, make several visits to the same place and capture it at different times of day. Make sure that you position the car to make best use of the light, and if you want to shoot the car from different angles you will probably need to move the car each time.

∨ The location here was a disused mine, and I used the broken window to frame the cars and to make the atmosphere of the location a part of the photograph. Run-down or derelict locations sometimes make a good contrast to exotic cars. **Renault Alpine (on left) and Lotus Europa, disused mine near Maidstone, Kent, England. Mamiya RB67, 50mm lens, Fuji Provia.**

∧ This was shot for a magazine feature about touring in a Bentley, and I deliberately chose to make the car only a small part of the scene. This was the best way of including the distinctive rock shapes but also helped to suggest the idea of driving the car through a beautiful landscape.
Bentley Continental, The Roaches, near Leek, Staffordshire, England. Mamiya RB67, 90mm lens, Fuji Provia.

road as part of the composition, and this is clearly an appropriate setting for almost any car. A deserted road winding across a hillside behind a car suggests freedom and driving pleasure, and this is the sort of image that advertisers often use to sell cars. Don't be afraid to make the car a small part of the picture if it works well this way.

It's not always possible, though, to take a car to a favoured location or landscape. A creative photographer can create stunning pictures out of familiar or ordinary surroundings, and this is the skill that you will need to acquire. Professional photographers who shoot cars often have to make the most of limited time and have to find

Making the most of the car

Cars are designed to be visually appealing, and every car has particular angles from which it will photograph well. Professional car photographers usually have to produce a portfolio of pictures that show various views of their subject, and are well versed in identifying the combination of viewpoint and lens that will highlight a car's shape to best effect. Often a combination of action and static images is used in a magazine feature to show various views of the car.

It is most common to shoot cars from a front three-quarter view; that is, looking at the car from one or other of the front corners. This is an angle that works well to show, in one image, the car's overall appearance. Sometimes it is best to use a low viewpoint when shooting from this angle, and unless you are after a particularly stylised shot it is best to avoid wide-angle lenses, as their exaggerated perspective tends to make the front of the car look excessively large. Medium telephoto lenses will usually suit this angle. Many photographers prefer to keep wheels in the 'straight ahead' position when shooting a front three-quarter view, but with some cars the wheels can be turned almost to the 'full lock' position (with the hub facing the

◁ To make the most of this famous and very valuable racing car, I placed the camera on the ground and used a waist-level viewfinder to compose the image. As it was a dull day I added flash (using a flashgun placed to the left of the car and connected to the camera with a long lead), which has emphasised the distinctive curves on the front of the car and picked out the spoked wheels. **Mercedes W125 racing car, airfield near Stuttgart, Germany. Mamiya RB67, 180mm lens, Metz 60CT-4 flash, Fuji Provia.**

The elegant curves of this Ferrari suited a rear three-quarter view, and I took care to position the car so that the light at dusk would make the most of the distinctive shape. The camera was just below eye level, as this meant that the line of the car's roof stood out against the field; if I had shot from lower down, the distant buildings, although out-of-focus, might have made a cluttered background. **Ferrari Daytona, near Porrentroy, Switzerland. Mamiya RB67, 180mm lens, 85B warm-up and graduated grey filters, Fuji Velvia.**

camera) to add interest. As well as shooting the traditional front three-quarter view, you should always aim to take a selection of other angles.

Some cars have distinctive rear views that make for great pictures, but pictures shot from straight behind a car are rarely flattering. Again it is much better to use a three-quarter view as this gives an impression of the overall shape, and it also worth checking to see if a viewpoint close to the ground suits the car. This is another situation where turning the front wheels can make a more interesting picture. The side profile view works well on many cars, but usually needs an uncluttered background to be successful. Make sure that the camera is placed level with the mid-point of the car to give the most natural-looking view, and always ensure that the wheels are straight. (Fussy photographers will make sure that any

logos or badges on wheel hubs are level, but unless the centres spin independently this is tricky to achieve.) It is sometimes worth looking for opportunities to shoot cars from above, as this is a view that is rarely seen but provides the best pictures of some cars.

As with all photography, attention to detail is important. It is of course essential to make sure that the car is spotlessly clean, and watch for any splashes of mud that may have appeared en route to the location. Make sure that anything in the car is well hidden, as a coat left draped across a seat back or a map on a rear shelf will spoil an otherwise good picture. Windows should be closed and sun visors should be in the 'up' position, and these are the sorts of details that are easy to miss at the time of shooting but will be obvious on the finished picture.

Here an upstairs window provided an opportunity to get this overhead view of a Lamborghini, and from this angle the various body details are clearly visible. Cars like this, that are very low and sleek, can be difficult to shoot well from low down and it is always worth looking out for unusual viewpoints. I used the shutter door and the windowsill to frame the car and deliberately kept them out-of-focus by using a wide aperture. **Lamborghini Countach LP400, near Sant'Agata, Italy. Mamiya RB67, 65mm lens, Fuji Provia.**

Engines

The engine is the heart of any car, and some are almost works of art and worthy of being photographed. The engines of many supercars or historic cars are complex constructions with masses of shiny metal that will naturally attract the keen photographer. Professional car photographers working for magazines always have to include an engine shot in the set of pictures of any significant car, but there is a particular skill in doing so successfully. The most difficult aspect of photographing an engine is making sure that the lighting is even, as in harsh lighting such as bright sunshine the end result will have far too much contrast, with bright highlights and very dark shadows.

The best way to ensure even lighting is to shoot in overcast conditions or find some shade, but even this does not guarantee good results; in the shade on a sunny day the light is very blue, and your pictures will have an unattractive blue cast unless you use a warm-up filter. (You could also consider using a gold reflector.) Position the car carefully, so that you make best use of the available light, and avoid shooting against the light if you can. Remember that some bonnets hinge at the front and some at the back, so bear this in mind before positioning the car. Every engine can be photographed from either side of the car, but there is always one view from which the engine will look more attractive. Usually the side with the exhaust manifolds clearly visible will be less interesting than the other side, but every

∨ The engine of this Bentley was a mass of shiny chrome and fine detail, and I chose to use a medium format camera and fine-grained film to do it justice. As the weather was overcast I could be sure that the lighting would be even with no harsh shadows, and I positioned the car carefully so that I had a plain background and no unwanted reflections in any of the chrome. **Bentley Speed Six, near Thame, Oxfordshire, England. Mamiya RB67, 65mm lens, Fuji Velvia.**

On a bright sunny day on an open road I couldn't find any shade in which to shoot the engine of this Maserati, so I added a fill-in flash to relieve the shadows. I chose to use an upright format and a wide-angle lens to include some of the scenery in the background. Most engines have one view that is better than the other and this side, showing the carburettors, made the more interesting picture. **Maserati A6G, Monaco. Mamiya RB67, 50mm lens, Metz 60CT-4 flash, Fuji Provia.**

engine is different, so use your own judgment. Many engines have the manufacturer's logo prominent on the cylinder head and it is sometimes possible to make this a feature of the picture. Avoid including any unsightly details in your shot; classic cars in particular look completely wrong when fitted with modern batteries, so always look out for this. Cleaning up a dirty engine bay can be a major undertaking, but sometimes a wipe with a rag can make a big difference.

The best viewpoint for many engine bays is from high up; consider standing on a camera case to gain a few extra inches. (Many professional car photographers never travel without a short stepladder, for situations like this.) Look for

an uncluttered background, although sometimes it is possible to include part of the surroundings as a feature of the picture.

Measure the light carefully, with a hand-held meter if you have one, as most engine bays appear very dark and this can easily lead the camera's exposure meter to over-expose. Always bracket the exposures to make sure. If it is difficult to find some shade, then an engine shot can sometimes be rescued by the addition of some fill-in flash. Again, the flashgun's sensor will be easily fooled into over-exposing, so make sure that the flash is set to give one or two stops less exposure than the aperture set on the lens, and shoot a series of frames using different aperture and flash settings.

It was difficult to get a good view of the engine of this Lamborghini, and shooting at night I chose a slightly abstract approach. I used flash and an exposure of ½ a second, hand-holding the camera, and after the flash had fired I deliberately moved the camera around to blur the lights on the distant buildings. **Lamborghini Diablo SV, London Docklands, England. Canon EOS1n, 24mm lens, Fuji Provia.**

Interiors

∨ It can be difficult to get a clear view of a car's interior. Here I used a wide-angle lens and carefully positioned the tripod so that I could include both the dashboard and the seats. I had carefully positioned the car so that the view through the windscreen contained no distracting detail. **MGA coupé, near Lichfield, Staffordshire, England. Canon EOS1n, 24mm lens, 81A warm-up filter, Fuji Provia.**

Many cars have beautiful interiors, with finely detailed dashboards adorned with leather or polished veneer, but taking good photographs of car interiors presents a real challenge. It is difficult to ensure even lighting, and many car interiors are very dark which makes hand-holding the camera impossible. A convertible or sports car interior, which can be photographed with the roof down, is of course much easier to shoot than that of a 'closed' car.

As with engine shots, shade or overcast light provide the best circumstances for shooting interiors. A wide-angle lens will probably be necessary to include the whole interior. You will need to position the car to make the best possible use of the available light; in particular avoid shooting against the light. (Opening a sunroof will increase the available light significantly.) Lighting car inter-

iors successfully with flash is difficult as the end result will tend to have excessive contrast, but you can sometimes use a small burst of flash as fill-in. If you have a powerful flashgun you can use a car's roof lining as a surface from which to bounce the flash, which provides soft, even lighting. A reflector is a useful accessory for shooting interiors. For an end result with good depth-of-field, you will need to set a small aperture and in the low light this often entails using a tripod, which is tricky in the confined space. Use a hand-held meter if you have one, as the light outside the car will cause a camera's meter to under-expose the interior.

Always try to find a plain background, as anything outside the car will be visible and may act as a distraction. It is usually best to shoot from outside the car with the door open, as this pro-

∨ To brighten up the interior of this BMW on a dull day I positioned a flash on a tripod on the far side of the car and opened the passenger door so that the dashboard and steering wheel would be evenly lit. I balanced the output of the flash carefully with the available light to produce a moody feel to the picture, and used instant film to check the flash was even and that there were no bright highlights or flare. **BMW 3.0CSi, near Llangollen, North Wales. Mamiya RB67, 50mm lens, Metz 60CT-4 flash, Fuji Provia.**

vides a good overall view of the interior. Choose between shooting from the driver's side or the passenger side according to the layout of the interior; alternatively sit in the back of the car and shoot looking to the front. Choose an angle that shows the dashboard at its best, and avoid shooting from a viewpoint where the steering wheel obscures significant details. Sometimes classic cars are fitted with modern radios that look completely out of place, and by careful selection of viewpoint you may be able to hide such distractions.

Make every effort to tidy the interior as much as possible. Remove maps, sunglasses, cassettes and so on, take out any additional floor mats (especially if they have picked up footmarks or muddy smears) and try to get rid of any dirt or leaves on the carpets. Most dashboards look less cluttered if you take the ignition keys out, and look carefully at the positions of any switches or dials to check they are neat. Always turn the steering wheel so that it sits straight, as it will look odd if turned to any other angle. Make sure sun visors are in the 'up' position, and adjust the front seats so that they are level with each other, as this always looks neater. Windows need to be free of smears or condensation, and most professional photographers prefer to remove tax discs and other stickers from windscreens for an uncluttered look.

◄ For the interior of this Corvette, I chose to make the background part of the image. I needed a tripod to ensure sufficient depth-of-field, and added a graduated grey filter to darken the distant landscape. Notice that the steering wheel is straight, and the seats and carpets clean.
Chevrolet Corvette Sting Ray, Brecon Beacons, South Wales. Mamiya RB67, 50mm lens, 85C warm-up and graduated grey filters, Fuji Velvia.

Details

Many cars – classic and vintage cars in particular – have fascinating details that make for good pictures. Look for badges, mascots, wheels or interesting design details, and go in close to isolate your subject. Make sure that you pay particular attention to the light, as good lighting will mean the difference between a competent picture and one that has real sparkle. This may mean moving the car just to change the angle of light on a tiny detail but the committed photographer will make the extra effort. As with all car photography, choose your time carefully as the beginning or the end of the day will undoubtedly provide the best light. Backgrounds are equally important – try to shoot in such a way that your subject has a clean background free of distracting elements, and look for colours and textures that will provide a contrast. Look for unusual viewpoints; sometimes you may need to kneel or lie on the ground to make the most of a detail shot or to remove an unwanted distraction from the background. Compare views of the subject from either side to see which works best according to the direction of the light. Sometimes, close-up details work well when covered with water droplets, and many professional photographers use a spray atomiser, like those sold in garden centres for watering house plants, to achieve this.

Close-up shots often require a macro lens, but don't worry if you don't have one, as most ordinary lenses will focus close enough to take good detail pictures. Most standard lenses will focus closer than telephoto or zoom lenses, even those that have 'macro' settings. Sometimes using a wide-angle lens from close in makes for really dramatic pictures, while many details look best when shot with a telephoto lens, as the compressed perspective helps to isolate the subject from the background. Whichever lens you use it is usually best to use the maximum aperture, keeping depth-of-field to a minimum, which helps to create a clean background. But take particular care with your focusing, as depth-of-field is very narrow anyway when the lens is used at its closest focus setting. Using auto-focus may help. Also be aware of the possibility of slight movement of a hand-held camera changing the point of focus. Using a wide aperture, and the corresponding fast shutter speed, helps to reduce the risk of camera shake.

Watch carefully for reflections, as it is easy for an unnoticed reflection of the photographer in a shiny chrome detail to ruin a good picture. If you are wearing bright clothing, watch that the colour is not reflected in your subject, creating a colour cast. This is a particular problem with white or silver cars or chrome badges. Make sure that the detail you're shooting, and the area around it, are clean – a soft cloth or piece of chamois leather is ideal for a final wipe before you press the shutter.

Look carefully at all these pictures and you will notice how, in each case, the light, focus and depth-of-field have been used in combination to create an attractive picture. Notice also how camera angles have been carefully chosen to make attractive compositions and to make the best use of backgrounds. All were shot using 35mm equipment and in each case exposures were bracketed to ensure a good result.

Multi-car groups 1

Shooting more than one car at a time is much more difficult than shooting individual cars, but professional car photographers often have to do this as so many magazine features are group tests or comparisons between rival models. It is always more difficult to find locations with space for more than one car, especially as with a car in the foreground and others behind there will need to be sufficient space between them for the more distant ones to be clearly visible.

It is important to find locations that are uncluttered and with clean backgrounds, as the individual shapes of each car need to be distinct. However, try to avoid using car parks as locations, as the painted white lines always spoil car pictures. Look for open spaces where you

◁ Placing cars in a V-formation often makes for a strong composition, but this usually works best with one car closer to the camera. Here I positioned the cars as the sun was setting and the colours in the sky became more and more spectacular as the evening progressed. By the time I took this it was virtually dark and an exposure of 15 seconds was necessary as I needed enough depth-of-field to keep both cars sharp. **Auto Union 1000 (in foreground) and Audi TT, near Aberdeen, Scotland. Mamiya RB67, 65mm lens, graduated grey and 85B warm-up filters, Fuji Velvia.**

composition out of two cars in a strict V-formation is hard. You could also try an arrangement where the two cars are at the same angle, parallel to each other, as this often makes the comparison between the shapes clear. For this type of shot a slightly higher viewpoint makes it easier to see the more distant car.

Another successful arrangement is to have the two cars facing in different directions, and again this nearly always works best with one car closer to the camera than the other. You will often need to spend a while moving the cars around until you have a visually pleasing arrangement, and keep checking through the camera to ensure that you have a good composition. Group shots where there are big gaps between the cars are rarely successful; always make sure that the cars form a compact set. In many cases it will not matter if the whole of each car is not visible, as it is far easier to make strong compositions where cars overlap. When composing group shots, always remember the basic rules of good composition and try to make sure that none of the cars is too close to the edge of the frame.

These two cars were shot for a magazine feature as they both have the same engine. I chose to place the cars at contrasting angles, and this helped to create a picture where the shapes of both cars were distinct. In general it is best to use brightly coloured cars in the foreground, and here the oilseed rape in the field added a splash of yellow that worked well with the red and green cars. **Maserati Merak (in foreground) and Citroën SM, near Royston, Hertfordshire, England. Mamiya RB67, 65mm lens, graduated grey filter, Fuji Velvia.**

Pictures like this often take a while to set up and involve a considerable time spent moving the cars small distances until the arrangement works. Here a slightly raised viewpoint was used as this made it easier to get a clear view of the two cars furthest from the camera. **Lancia Appia Series 1 (foreground) Series 3 (middle) and Series 2, near Oxford, England. Mamiya RB67, 65mm lens, graduated tobacco filter, Fuji Provia.**

can move cars into any formation that you choose and where the choice of viewpoints is not compromised. Composing group shots needs a great deal of care, and the most difficult aspect of this is positioning the cars in an attractive formation.

Cars one in front of another in a straight line will look as though they are parked rather than arranged for a picture and in any case it is hard to make a strong image out of an arrangement like this. Two cars often work well when placed in a V-arrangement, although the camera position has to be chosen carefully to make the most of this. It is usually preferable to have one car closer to the camera than the other, as making a strong

Multi-car groups 2

When shooting groups of cars it will often be useful to use a high viewpoint as this makes it easier to see the more distant cars clearly. Many professional photographers carry stepladders for situations like this. Some also have roof racks on their cars that are strong enough to support the

◁ Here a steep hillside provided a viewpoint that gave a clear view of all three cars, and I chose to position them in such a way that their distinctive rears were all visible. This was shot on a winter's day at a popular spot on the Dorset coast; at other times of the year it is extremely unlikely that this site would be free of other cars. I switched on the cars' hazard lights to brighten up the picture. **Ferrari 308 (on left), Lotus Esprit (centre) and De Tomaso Pantera, Kimmeridge, Dorset, England. Mamiya RB67, 90mm lens, graduated tobacco and 85C warm-up filters, Fuji Velvia.**

For this picture I arranged the cars so that all faced away from a central point and then chose a camera position from which each car's shape was distinct. As it was overcast (and raining) I asked the drivers to turn on the cars' sidelights, which brightened up the picture, and I also made sure that the brightest coloured car was in the foreground.
Left to right: BMW 850 Csi, BMW 3.0 CSi and BMW 635 CSi, near Llangollen, North Wales. Mamiya RB67, 65mm lens, graduated grey filter, Fuji Provia.

weight of a photographer and tripod. It helps if you can find a location where you can gain some additional height, for example by climbing a bank, or using a staircase or upstairs window. The more cars in the group you are shooting, the higher you will need to be if you wish to have an uninterrupted view of each.

Big groups of cars are difficult to arrange in attractive formations so position cars that sit low to the ground in the foreground, as this will make it easier to see the further distant ones. Lens choice is also important; use a wide-angle lens for a group shot and the cars close to the camera will take over the composition while more distant ones may end up too small in the frame. For this reason standard lenses often work best for multiple car shots, while it will be very difficult to use a telephoto lens successfully for groups of more than two cars.

Depth-of-field is an important consideration; you will need to use an aperture small enough to keep all the cars in the group sharp. Check carefully using the depth-of-field preview if your camera has one, or use the scale on the lens. Remember that one-third of the total depth-of-

field extends towards the camera from the point of focus, while the other two-thirds extends away from the camera. Use this fact to choose your point of focus and aperture to maximise the depth-of-field. Small apertures mean long shutter speeds and this brings the risk of camera shake. You will almost certainly need to use a tripod, and with this at its fullest extension, as is often necessary with group shots, you will need to take particular care. Use a cable release to reduce vibration and be especially careful in high winds.

When arranging cars for group shots, always take care with the arrangement of the different colours. Cars that are bright red or yellow should be in the foreground to create a picture that has immediate visual impact, but it is important to ensure that dark cars are not lost in the background. Where more than one car in the group share the same colour, endeavour to place them in different parts of the picture. Always try to position cars in such a way that they make best use of the light; in circumstances where there are areas of light and shade ensure that all the cars are in the brighter parts of the scene.

Large groups of cars are very difficult to arrange into attractive fromations. Here I started by positioning the cars in the foreground and then asking the drivers to move all the others, one at a time, into the obvious spaces towards the back. Each was placed at an angle that would complement those of the cars nearby, and it was important to make sure that the gaps between the cars were even.
Bristol 403 (foreground left), 400 (extreme right) and various other Bristol cars, Goodwood, West Sussex, England. Mamiya RB67, 65mm lens, graduated grey filter, Fuji Provia.

Including people

Straightforward images of cars on their own can sometimes be a little lifeless, and including one or more people is a good way of adding interest and creating a livelier picture. Adding a pretty girl to a car is an obvious ploy that has long been used in manufacturers' brochures (and at motor shows), and magazines often use the same method to boost sales. Many classic cars also offer the potential for 'themed' costume shoots, using appropriate locations, which can be great fun to do.

◁ For a feature on this Lotus Elan, a professional model was booked to liven up the pictures on a dull day. She was asked to bring a selection of clothes and footwear suitable for a 1970s car, and the green top was selected as it made a good contrast with the yellow car. I tilted the camera slightly to create a stronger composition. Two flashguns added a subtle hint of sparkle, and a warm-up filter was used to give a more pleasing tone to the picture.
Lotus Elan, test track at Crowthorne, Berkshire, England. Mamiya RB67, 180mm lens, graduated grey and 81C warm-up filters, Metz 60CT-4 and 45CT-5 flashguns, Fuji Provia.

The main difficulty of including people in car shoots is creating a good composition. People standing up usually suit an upright format, while cars suit a landscape format. It can be tricky to make a strong composition, without a lot of empty space, that suits both subjects. It sometimes helps to find a high viewpoint, looking down on the car, which solves the problem. Otherwise consider going in close, even cropping off part of the car if necessary. When you include people in your picture, they will usually be the focal point and you should focus on the person rather than on the car. However, there will be occasional exceptions to this rule, such as when you are using a person as part of a composition rather than as the main subject.

Professional photographers are often able to work with paid models, who are used to posing for cameras and are readily able to adopt natural-looking stances and expressions. Other people, though, will always be self-conscious in front of a camera and you will need to try to put them at ease. It helps to shoot plenty of

pictures, as it is often the case that people become more relaxed as the shoot goes on. (It is also frustrating to find, as often happens, that your subject has blinked at the precise instant that the shutter was open, on what would otherwise have been the best picture; shooting a few extra frames helps avoid this.) Always make sure that your subject is comfortable, as anyone who is cold, or standing or sitting in an awkward position, is unlikely to look good on the finished picture. On a cold or windy day it often helps to have a warm coat to hand that the subject can slip on between shots. A warm-up filter is a useful accessory when shooting any people pictures, as it makes skin tones look a healthier colour.

Ask your subject to wear clothes that match the car, not just in terms of colour but also that look appropriate for the age and style of the car. Attention to detail is essential here: a model wearing, for example, a modern wristwatch, might spoil an otherwise good picture of a classic or veteran car.

Costume shoots

Classic cars can be used, along with models, props, costumes and appropriate locations, for 'themed' shoots that recreate the feel of a particular era. Research is important here – find out the age of the car and identify the types of clothing, hairstyle and props that will work. Some cars are especially identified with particular periods – Minis or E-type Jaguars typify the 'swinging Sixties', for example – and you can use this as a basis for your pictures. Other cars might have been popular with particular professions or classes of society and this might provide the inspiration for a costume shoot.

Choose a location that matches the period of the car. This is increasingly difficult but the wonders of digital manipulation make it easy to remove distracting non-period details, such as road signs or wall-mounted alarm boxes, on the computer later. Look for streets with houses built

in the car's era (and that haven't had modern double glazing fitted), or old-fashioned shop fronts. Think about the places where the car would frequently have been seen in its time, and that will make good backgrounds for striking pictures. The biggest problem will often be finding a location that isn't crowded with modern cars; you could try shooting at quiet times, such as early on a Sunday morning or late on a summer evening.

Try to find models who will look 'right' and who will be comfortable dressing up and acting out roles. Suitable friends or relatives might be persuaded that a day out posing for pictures will be fun, but make sure that you work quickly and efficiently to prevent your models from getting bored. Ask your subjects to imagine they are the people they are portraying, and to act out the roles they are playing. Get them to engage in conversation and to make hand gestures as they

For a magazine feature on these 1930s Morrises, we were lucky to be allowed the use of a golf course as a location. We shot on a weekday morning when there were few players around, and worked out a set of pictures using different parts of the course where there were no obvious modern features in the background. The clubs and bags were borrowed from a display in the clubhouse, while the models were a husband and wife and a friend, who interacted naturally with each other. The outfits were assembled by borrowing from various sources, including the models' own wardrobes.
Morris Special Coupés: Minor (left) and Isis, golf club near Maldon, Essex, England. Mamiya RB67, 65mm lens, Fuji Provia.

This Rover was a popular choice with civil servants in its day and this was used as the basis for the photo shoot. The car's owner played the role of chauffeur, while the 'civil servants' were friends of the magazine's staff, chosen as they looked right. All the locations are in the centre of London and the only way we could hope to get the pictures was to shoot late on a June evening, when these areas were largely deserted, and it was important to work quickly as parking was restricted at each site.
Rover P4, central London, England. Mamiya RB67, 65mm and 90mm lenses, 85A warm-up filter, Fuji Provia.

talk, as this always makes for more realistic-looking pictures and avoids people looking too 'wooden'. Period clothing can be hired from theatrical costumiers, and will always look the part, but this is an expensive luxury that is really only available to professional photographers. Charity shops can be a useful alternative, as can older relatives who have attics full of old clothes! Similarly you may have to beg or borrow appropriate items to use as props, but the more period details you can find the more authentic your pictures will look.

Have a list of shots that you want to achieve and work through them, allocating a set amount of time for each. But be prepared to alter the schedule if the weather changes unexpectedly, or if new ideas occur to you as you work. If you have persuaded friends or relatives to act as models, always make sure that you supply them with some of the pictures afterwards in return for their help. This gesture also helps to ensure future goodwill from anyone who has lent props or clothes, or allowed the use of their property as a location.

Shows and events

It is often the case that the only opportunities to get up close to interesting and unusual cars are at organised events such as car shows. Circumstances like these present numerous difficulties for the photographer, in particular a lack of control – you will have to get your shots without being able to move the car, and you will often have to cope with crowds of people, and unfavourable lighting conditions. Car shows are always popular and if you want to take good pictures you will need to choose your time carefully. Arrive early in the morning before the crowds arrive or be prepared to wait until the end of the day. The latter approach enables you to wander around the show and decide which cars you wish to photograph, and then shoot

◁ Getting a clear shot of this concept car was a real challenge; first I had to obtain permission to move a rope from in front of the car, taking care that it did not obstruct the passage of other visitors, and then wait for people to move out of the way. With the camera on a tripod, I took a meter reading in advance and as soon as the background was clear I shot a sequence of frames, bracketing the exposures. Fortunately there was plenty of daylight filtering through the glass roof and I was able to work without flash.
Renault Vel Satis concept car, Renault museum, Paris, France. Canon EOS1n, 35mm lens, 81A warm-up filter, Fuji Provia.

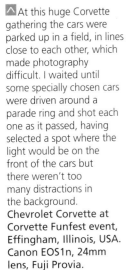

At this huge Corvette gathering the cars were parked up in a field, in lines close to each other, which made photography difficult. I waited until some specially chosen cars were driven around a parade ring and shot each one as it passed, having selected a spot where the light would be on the front of the cars but there weren't too many distractions in the background.
Chevrolet Corvette at Corvette Funfest event, Effingham, Illinois, USA. Canon EOS1n, 24mm lens, Fuji Provia.

when there are fewer people (and, outdoors, the light will probably be better). Weekends will always be the most popular time for visitors so if you are able to visit on a weekday you will stand more chance of shooting uncluttered pictures.

Patience is an essential virtue when shooting at shows, as there will almost always be people wandering through the shot when you wish to press the shutter. Sometimes you may have to wait a long time for a slot when there's no-one around, and in some situations you will have to put up with people in the background; take care at least to ensure that anyone with bright clothing or a silly hat has moved on, as they will tend to be the focal point of your picture. At car shows where owners have brought their cars along, you may be able to arrange with the owner to take some pictures when the event is over, and this may provide the opportunity to choose a clean background or at least to move the car to a more favourable angle for the prevailing light.

Cars at shows are often parked together and it is difficult to find a viewpoint where

you can get a clear view of the car. Distracting backgrounds are often a problem as well. You could try shooting from low down or finding a way of looking down on the car, as both approaches often make for stronger pictures. Another problem is that barriers and ropes are often used to keep visitors away from cars and these will spoil your picture. If you ask you may be allowed to move them out of the way while you take your picture, but you will have to work quickly and avoid inconveniencing other visitors. Ask also if you can briefly remove 'Please Do Not Touch' signs or other distractions. Watch also for items of litter that will ruin your picture – a stray crisp packet will inevitably stand out on the finished image.

While it is always preferable to use a tripod – and indoors it may be essential – there are many situations where they are either forbidden or impractical (such as at a packed motor show). You could ask for special permission, but otherwise you could try bracing against a pillar or a wall to help eliminate the risk of camera shake.

To get this shot of a Ferrari dealer's stand at a motor show I waited until almost closing time, then set the camera up on a tripod and waited until there was no-one on the stand. Lighting the whole group of cars with flash would have been difficult so I relied on the available light, and although the tungsten lamps have given the film a yellow cast this works well with the red cars to create a picture that feels 'warm'. Using tungsten-balanced film or print film, or a digital camera, would have eliminated the cast.
Ferrari Dino (left) Daytona (blue car at rear) 275GTB (centre), 250 California (white car at rear) and 250SWB (right) at London Motor Show, Earl's Court, London. Canon EOS1n, 24mm lens, Fuji Provia.

Shooting indoors

The biggest difficulty when shooting indoors at motor shows or museums is the lighting. There is usually little available light and most flashguns simply aren't powerful enough to illuminate an entire car. (The flash will 'fall off' just a few feet from the camera, so while the front of the car may be correctly exposed the rest of the scene will be under-exposed.) The solution is to combine flash and available light, and while this requires a degree of technical understanding it is the best way to achieve successful results. First you will need to establish the correct exposure for the available light; in most indoor situations light levels are sufficiently low to require the use of a tripod, and it is not unusual for shutter speeds of up to one second to be necessary.

Most professional photographers use hand-held meters to measure the exposure in tricky situations like these, but your camera's meter will work just as well as you are only using the read-

◁ In this museum interior there was plenty of available light but as most of it was coming from behind the car I added flash from the right-hand side of the shot to retain detail in that side of the car. I took an exposure reading with a hand-held meter and set the flashgun to under-expose by one stop so that it would act as 'fill-in' rather than as the main light source. This area was also lit by several fluorescent lights, but I managed to arrange for these to be switched off while I took this shot, to avoid any trace of a green cast.
Benetton Renault B197, Renault museum, Paris, Canon EOS1n, 35mm lens, Metz 60CT-4 flashgun, 81A warm-up filter, Fuji Provia.

>These two pictures illustrate the effect of combining flash with available light. Using the flash as the main light, an exposure of 1/60th of a second at f/5.6 resulted in a dark background and uneven lighting on the car. I then took a reading from the background and adjusted the camera settings to ½ of a second at f/5.6, leaving the flash set to f/5.6. The bright highlight on the metal door is also less noticeable on the shot with the brighter background. **Mercedes-Benz 500K Roadster, Mercedes-Benz museum, Stuttgart, Germany. Canon EOS1n, 24mm lens, Metz 60CT-4 flash, Fuji Provia.**

ing as a guide. Let's assume that your meter comes up with an exposure of ½ a second at f/4. You should then set your flashgun to give a correct exposure at f/4, but set the camera's controls to ¼ of a second at f/4. That way you will be slightly under-exposing the background (this will keep any colour cast to a minimum) but preventing it from going too dark (which it would if you relied on the flashgun and shot at, say, 1/30th of a second at f/4).

The combination of the flash and available light should produce a good result, but it is always worth bracketing the exposures to be sure. Try changing both the shutter speed and the flash setting, and bear in mind that white or dark cars may fool flashgun sensors into under-

or over-exposing. Remember also that, from a creative point of view, the worst position for a flashgun is on the camera, so try to at least hold the flash at arm's length using an extension lead. Many hand-held meters have a facility for measuring flash exposures, and this can help you to ensure a good result.

You can still use this flash-and-available-light technique in situations where it is impossible to use a tripod, as the flash will at least ensure that the area close to the camera is free of camera shake, but hold the camera as steady as possible, or your background will be excessively blurred.

There are some indoor environments where the available light is much better, but even in a situation where there is plenty of daylight from a glass roof it may be useful to add a burst of 'fill-in' flash to retain detail in the car. In some circumstances – such as when trying to include several cars in one shot – it may be preferable to rely entirely on the available light, but always be alert to the possibility of colour casts. Fluorescent lighting in particular imparts an unsightly green cast on transparency film, so consider using filters or switching to print materials. Most digital cameras have an automatic 'white balance' feature that will adjust to cope with almost any light source.

^This car museum was lit entirely by fluorescent lighting so I fitted a magenta colour conversion filter to correct the green cast. I needed to use a tripod and a shutter speed of ¼ of a second, but the fluorescent lights do provide even illumination that works well with cars. **Maserati 420 M58, museum at Bassano del Grappa, Italy. Canon EOS1n, 24mm lens, CC30M filter, Fuji Provia.**

Finding cars for photography

Most of us own relatively ordinary cars, and while it is perfectly possible to take good pictures of any car it is more exciting to photograph exotic sports cars, or beautiful classics. So how can we arrange to shoot more interesting cars, in situations of our choosing rather than at car shows? And how do magazines get regular access to brand new cars, and to top-of-the-range performance machines?

Car magazines that feature the latest models have access to fleets of press cars maintained by the manufacturers and supplied on loan for road testing and photography, and professional photographers have the luxury of being able to take these cars to their choice of location, and to favourite roads and test tracks. Those magazines that specialise in classic or custom cars have to rely on generous owners (contacted via the net-

For access to cars like this rare and very valuable Bugatti, car magazines rely on the generosity of wealthy owners who are prepared to loan their cars for photo shoots. Here a private test track was used so that the car could be driven in safety, and I had to work quickly to keep the distances driven to a minimum. Notice that the driver is wearing clothing appropriate to the car. Bugatti Type 43, test track near Chobham, Surrey, England. Nikon F3, 35mm lens, Fuji Provia.

It's not necessary to use expensive or rare cars for good pictures; here a humble Mini was the subject and the strength of the image relies on careful timing and composition. The car was positioned on the brow of a hill that gave a clear view of the sunset, and I asked the driver to turn on the headlights to avoid it becoming a pure silhouette.
Mini Cooper, Burton Dassett Hills, Warwickshire, England. Nikon F3, 70–200mm lens, Fuji Velvia.

work of owners' clubs), or dealers who are prepared to lend cars from their stock for photo shoots. Both owners and dealers are prepared to do this because there is a certain kudos to having a car featured in a magazine, and its value may increase slightly as a result, but cars usually have to be photographed at locations close to the car's home base, and driven carefully. Neither owners nor dealers are likely to be so helpful when approached by a keen amateur who simply wants to take pictures for their own collections. And you will certainly not be given the keys to an exotic supercar and allowed to drive around for the day on the pretext of taking photographs.

Nonetheless, if you adopt the right methods you may find owners who are willing to allow you to take pictures of their cars. A polite approach, with a careful explanation of what you have in mind, will often pay dividends. It helps if you are able to show some examples of your work, and offer to provide a set of the resulting pictures to the owner. (Make sure that you fulfil this offer.) You could visit classic car shows or owners' club gatherings with your portfolio and ask around. Sometimes a polite note left on a

windscreen, with a telephone number, will lead to a positive response. You are more likely to be successful if you have a location in mind for your photo shoot, near to the owners' home, and you will also have to be flexible about date and time. Do not expect that anyone is going to let you drive his or her car; explain that you are only interested in taking pictures and arrange that they will meet you at your choice of location at a pre-arranged time. The owner of a valuable car will undoubtedly be suspicious about strangers asking to photograph his or her car, and you will have to be prepared for your approach to be unsuccessful.

An alternative option is to hire a car for photography. As well as the mainstream hire companies (some of which have exotic cars in their ranges), there are a growing number of specialist companies who hire classic and performance cars. Many of these companies advertise in the motoring press. If you want to hire a Ferrari or Lamborghini for the weekend you will have to pay handsomely for the privilege, but there are many more modest classics available, most of which will make excellent subjects for photography.

Cars lent by owners often have to be photographed close to the owner's home. Here I decided to use the sea front and beach huts as a background and the winter sunlight helped to make a striking picture.
Mercedes-Benz 450SLC, Frinton-on-Sea, Essex, England. Mamiya RB67, 65mm lens, graduated grey filter, Fuji Velvia.

Preparing the car

Professional car photographers spend a lot of time preparing cars for photo shoots. This means not just cleaning the car, but making sure that it looks as original and uncluttered as possible. Look through car magazines and you will notice that cars are rarely photographed with the windows down, or with stickers on the windscreen; it is attention to small details like this that can make all the difference to a successful picture.

It goes almost without saying that a car should

◀ The state of the roads during the winter months makes photography especially difficult. On a January day this Morgan had to be repeatedly cleaned between locations, especially as any marks or streaks would have been obvious on the cream paintwork. I was lucky to find a section of road that was relatively clean, which avoided the need to clean the car between 'passes', but that also had a good background (and where the car was in full sunlight). **Morgan Plus 8, near Malvern, Worcestershire, England. Nikon F3, 70–200mm lens, Fuji Velvia.**

△It is often only necessary to clean those parts of the car that are clearly visible. After a hasty drive around to find a location for this shot the car had picked up a great deal of dirt from the wet roads, but the light was fading fast. There was only time to clean those parts of the car facing the camera, and the areas in shadow were given only a cursory wipe. In the low light it was difficult to see any remaining marks clearly through the camera and I had to check the car carefully from close in.
Aston Martin Virage, near Norwich, Norfolk, England. Mamiya RB67, 65mm lens, graduated grey and 85A warm-up filters, Fuji Provia.

be spotlessly clean before any pictures are taken. This means not just a thorough clean and polish before setting off but also frequent checks and more cleaning. Professional photographers include in their equipment buckets, sponges, chamois leathers, rolls of kitchen paper, wax polish, spray cleaners for windows and tyres and even pump sprayers (like those used by gardeners), and often spend more time on a shoot cleaning the car than taking pictures. For the initial clean, a 'jet wash' is usually more effective than a drive-through car wash, as it allows particular attention to be paid to areas like wheels and sills that quickly get dirty out on the road. On a winter's day, a photographer may end up jet-washing the car several times during the course of a shoot as well as frequently wiping off any dirt picked up on the road. As well as a thorough clean, it is worth using specialised glass cleaning fluid for windows (this helps to remove smears), and the substances available for dressing tyres (which ensure tyres have a deep black colour).

Most professional photographers will remove road tax discs and other stickers from windscreens, which makes the car look a lot neater.

The UK tax disc has the date clearly visible and as this dates the picture it limits the useful life of the image. Cars also look much better with all the windows closed; this is how the designer intended the car to be seen and open windows spoil the 'line' of the car. Radio aerials should also be in the fully retracted position, as they spoil the shape of the car. Check that both sun visors are in the 'up' position (and keep rechecking, as flipping down the sun visor is an instinctive reaction for most drivers, even if only moving the car a few metres for a photographer). Some owners adorn their cars with badge bars, or aftermarket accessories that spoil a car's originality. If possible, tactfully ask about removing these but you may have to choose a camera angle that disguises them or minimises their visual impact. Watch for anything left inside the car that is visible from outside, and tuck it out of the way. Always look very carefully at any reflections in the car's bodywork, chrome or door mirrors; more than one photographer has examined their results only to see a perfect reflection of their own car, complete with camera bags and cleaning materials.

△Details like spoked wheels can be particularly tricky to clean; here the car's owner had spent a great deal of time cleaning the car prior to the shoot and had used special cleaners for both the wheels and tyres, making it easy to shoot detail shots like this.
Aston Martin DB4 GT, Goodwood, West Sussex. Mamiya RB67, 180mm lens, Fuji Provia.

Studio photography

Many of the car photographs in advertisements and magazines are shot in studios, and while few amateur photographers are likely to have the opportunity to shoot in such places it is useful to know how professional photographers work in the studio environment.

Most studios large enough to accommodate cars have what is known as an 'infinity cove'. This is a studio space in which all the intersections between the floor and the walls, and between the walls themselves, are curved. Standing in an infinity cove is disconcerting as it impossible to judge the distances to the walls, and this is of course precisely the intention; on the finished photograph the background behind the car appears as an area of plain white (or whatever other colour is chosen). Few professional car photographers have their own stu-dios; most infinity coves are run as hire facilities and are booked when needed. Coves are usual-ly painted white as this gives a good clean background from which the car can be 'cut out' in the reproduction process, but some briefs call for other colours and many studios employ assistants who spend most of their time repainting the cove (and in any case a white cove needs regular re-painting to hide tyre marks and so on).

The most challenging aspect of shooting cars in the studio is lighting. To look their best cars need to be lit with soft, even lighting with no harsh highlights and this can take many hours of careful adjustment (and frequent checks with instant films) to achieve. Tungsten lights, which have a continuous output, are often preferred to flash as the effect of any adjustment can be seen

▽ A great deal of time and effort is needed to produce a picture like this. Notice that although the lighting is even the distinctive curves and lines are still evident, and also note that there are no unsightly reflections, even in the shiny chrome hubcaps. **Citroën DS in an infinity cove studio. Sinar 5x4 camera, 360mm lens, Fuji RTP tungsten film.**

immediately. The lights are usually reflected from walls, ceiling and large panels (known as 'flats') rather than shone directly on to the car. Cars lit with totally even light can sometimes look rather dull and photographers often use large pieces of black cloth to provide interesting patterns of reflection across the roof or sides. For advertising purposes, cars are often shot in studios and then 'stripped in' to location photographs (as this is cheaper and easier than setting up an entire shoot in, say, the Sahara Desert) and in such cases particular care has to be taken to ensure that the lighting on the car matches that of the location shot exactly.

Moving cars around in the studio is difficult and time-consuming and once the subject is parked on the cove minor adjustments are made by using 'skates'. These are sets of small wheels that are clamped to a car's tyres and which allow it to be easily moved. Compared with shooting on location, the studio is a very unforgiving environment and particular care has to be taken with cleaning and polishing the car, as even specks of dust will be clearly visible under the even lighting. Unwanted reflections can be difficult to hide in the limited circumstances of a studio and 'dulling spray' is often used to disguise these. Other tricks

of the trade include stacking bricks or sandbags in the boot of a car to give it a lower, sleeker profile, or taping pieces of cloth across the rear wall of the studio to retain a clearly visible edge on a light-coloured car.

▲Although this picture was shot to be used as a cut-out, including the entire image shows some of the techniques used by the photographer. The black cloth draped across the background provided the attractive areas of light and dark across the windscreen, and a similar technique was used for the distinct line along the car's body. A reflector used to brighten the front of the car is just visible on the right-hand edge of the picture. **Porsche 911 in an infinity cove studio, Sinar 5x4 camera, 360mm lens, Fuji RTP tungsten film.**

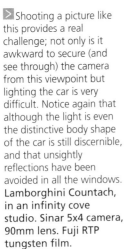 

▷Shooting a picture like this provides a real challenge; not only is it awkward to secure (and see through) the camera from this viewpoint but lighting the car is very difficult. Notice again that although the light is even the distinctive body shape of the car is still discernible, and that unsightly reflections have been avoided in all the windows. **Lamborghini Countach, in an infinity cove studio. Sinar 5x4 camera, 90mm lens. Fuji RTP tungsten film.**

Selling your work

Sooner or later most amateur photographers seek to recoup some of the expense of their hobby by selling their pictures, and there is a real thrill in seeing one's work in print. While there are various potential markets for car pictures, it is important to understand the exact requirements of each and to ensure that any work submitted matches those requirements.

Newsagents' shelves are crammed with motoring publications and it is easy to think of this a huge potential market for pictures, but the reality is that selling uncommissioned work to car magazines is very difficult. Most of the pictures used in features are shot by staff photographers or commissioned from freelances, and many of those used to illustrate news items or other sections are obtained from stock libraries or press releases. Magazine contents are planned and prepared a long time in advance and there is little room for work submitted 'on spec'. Some of the magazines that include coverage of motorsport and car shows rely on freelance contributors for those sections and you may be able to sell pictures of such events. It helps if you can provide text as well as pictures and your work will have to be submitted very quickly as magazines work to strict deadlines.

◁ There are a great many photographers covering motorsport events and hoping to sell their work, and it is worth making the effort to take unusual pictures if you want your work to stand out. Here I combined flash and a long exposure to create an image that had plenty of movement, but such pictures are not to every editor's taste and any submission should include some straightforward shots as well as abstract ones. **Lotus Cortina, on Pirelli Classic Marathon near Cortina, Italy. Nikon F3, 35mm lens, Metz 60CT-4 flash, Fuji Provia.**

Many publishers and picture libraries favour images that have a clear view of the car in a simple, uncluttered setting. While this approach limits creativity, those photographers who understand their markets, and shoot accordingly, register many more sales than those who insist on a personal 'style' of image. **Bentley Speed Six, near Watlington, Oxfordshire, England. Mamiya RB67, 180mm lens, Fuji Velvia.**

Bear in mind that there are many other freelances out there who are also looking to exploit the same markets, and many already have good working relationships with several magazines. Because there are so many people shooting at car events, publishers pay low rates for such pictures and you will be lucky if the income from picture sales covers the costs incurred in attending an event. If you have pictures (or an idea) that you think might interest an editor then a brief letter or e-mail outlining what you have should be the initial approach; editors are busy people and do not take kindly to phone calls from hopeful freelances. Always make sure you are familiar with the magazine you are looking to sell work to – there is little point in trying to sell pictures of classic cars to a magazine that features only the latest models.

Stock libraries are another potential source of income. These sell work on behalf of a photographer and the income is split, usually on a 50/50 basis (although many libraries are now asking for 60 per cent). While this may seem excessive, it is worth bearing in mind that libraries are the first port of call for many picture buyers, and most have access to markets all over the world that it would otherwise be very difficult for the photographer to exploit. (And 50 per cent of a lot of sales is better than 100 per cent of a few.) There are some libraries that specialise in automotive images and it is much better to lodge work with a library that knows a particular market well than with one that has millions of images on a variety of subjects. Look at the various libraries' websites to ascertain which might be interested in your work. Most libraries require large initial submissions and frequent additional ones, and insist on keeping pictures for a number of years to market them properly, and you should only submit work of the very highest technical and pictorial quality.

Finally, there are greetings card and calendar publishers who specialise in motoring subjects and may be a potential market for car pictures. Unfortunately, as any browse through the cards and calendars on sale will reveal, most of these companies have very conservative tastes and require rather dull, formulaic pictures.

Some photographers specialise in selling pictures to motorsport participants. It is important to make sure that you shoot every car in an event, preferably from different angles, and you will need to have proofs available quickly for participants to order from. Many of those shooting this work have turned to digital cameras, as the pictures can be viewed immediately on a laptop computer and then prints made, on location, in minutes. **Jaguar D-type at Goodwood race circuit, West Sussex. Canon EOS1n, 300mm lens, Fuji Provia.**

Shooting cars for a living

To many people, being paid to take pictures of cars seems a dream lifestyle. The reality, of course, is rather different – professional car photographers work long hours, spend inordinate amounts of time travelling up and down motorways and often have to work in pouring rain or freezing cold yet still come up with outstanding results. They need to come up with a constant stream of original and creative ideas for car pictures, yet at the same time have the technical skills to produce sharp, perfectly exposed pictures on every assignment. In addition, most photographers rarely, if ever, get to drive any of the exotic machinery they shoot. Car photography is a crowded profession and as a result only a very

few talented and hard-working individuals earn large amounts of money exclusively from motoring work. Nonetheless most professionals get to travel extensively, often have privileged access to cars and situations that few members of the public get to see, and it can be an exciting and challenging career.

There are various routes for the aspiring professional photographer to choose: some manage to find work as photographers' assistants, and while this is a good 'hands-on' introduction wages are low and the work often involves long hours performing menial tasks. Few car photographers working in the editorial field can afford an assistant but this is the best route for those

▽Professional car photographers need to have a good knowledge of locations and of suitable roads for driving pictures; most keep a stock of maps with good sites clearly marked. Here a favourite road across Dartmoor was used in the evening when there was little traffic and a tracking shot could be done in safety, and when the light was attractive. **Triumph TR5, Dartmoor, Devon, England. Canon EOS1n, 35mm lens, Fuji Velvia.**

▲ Photo shoots for magazines have to go ahead even in poor weather, and the professional photographer needs to produce good results in any conditions. Shooting a dark grey car on a dull day was a real challenge, and I managed to find a stretch of road with a good background but where I could still use the overcast light to highlight the distinctive shape of the car.
Jaguar Mk II, near Bridgnorth, Shropshire. Nikon F3, 70–200mm lens, Fuji Provia.

who wish to work in advertising. Some attend college courses in photography, either full- or part-time, but this is by no means a guarantee of a career and only a small percentage of college leavers end up working as photographers.

Unlike most other publications, many car magazines now employ staff photographers. This is largely because the amount of time photographers spend travelling to and from shoots, both at home and abroad, makes the regular use of freelances an expensive proposition. These jobs are occasionally advertised but each post has huge numbers of applicants, and as wages are generally low this work tends to appeal to young photographers embarking on their careers. Most see staff jobs as stepping stones to freelance careers, and spend a few years improving their skills as a staff member before moving on to work for themselves.

There are a great many freelance photographers attempting to make a living from car work,

and even though there are so many motoring publications it is surprisingly difficult to break into this field. Even those magazines that have staff photographers regularly use freelances as well, but most rely on a small number with whom they have established working relationships. This is because an editor needs to be sure that if he sends a photographer on an assignment he can rely on getting good results, no matter what constraints the weather, the location or the time available place on the photographer. An unknown photographer who has a portfolio of outstanding pictures might have spent a very long time on each one and may simply not be able to cope when asked to produce enough pictures for a magazine feature in a limited time. Some freelances who have acquired good reputations also shoot publicity work for car manufacturers; this often pays better than editorial work but offers the photographer a lesser degree of creative freedom.

▲ As well as being able to recognise the potential for creative pictures, it is important to have the technical skills to capture them on film. A subject like a glass mascot is tricky to expose correctly and I had to position the car in such as way as to make use of the light source in the background. I used a long lens and a wide aperture to make sure the mascot stood out from its surroundings.
Mascot on Rolls-Royce Phantom III, central London, England. Nikon F3, 70–200mm lens, Fuji Provia.

Index